Wings of War

Wings of War

Two First Hand Accounts of Pilots During the First World War

The Airman

C. Mellor

and

"Brother Bosch"

Gerald Featherstone Knight

LEONAUR

Wings of War
Two First Hand Accounts of Pilots During the First World War
The Airman
by C. Mellor
and
"Brother Bosch"
by Gerald Featherstone Knight

First published under the titles
The Airman
and
"Brother Bosch"

Leonaur is an imprint
of Oakpast Ltd

ISBN: 978-1-78282-068-0 (hardcover)
ISBN: 978-1-78282-069-7 (softcover)

http://www.leonaur.com

Contents

The Airman

Contents

Note

The original title of this book was *"The Air Pilot."* It was, however, found that this title had already been taken in America. It was therefore changed at the last moment to *"The Airman."*

Introduction
By Maurice Farman.

Paris, le 23 mars, 1913.

Cher Monsieur Mellor,

Je viens de lire votre ouvrage sur l'art de devenir aviateur et je ne saurais vous dire combien il m'a interessé.

Les lecteurs y trouveront relaté d'une façon claire et précise ce qu'il faut faire pour commencer à savoir voler, et aussi, ce qui peut être plus important encore, "tout ce qu'il ne faut pas faire."

Ils y trouveront aussi dérits d'une façon tout à fait pittoresque les amusants à côtés de la vie de l'élève aviateur qui sont reservés aux amateurs de ce nouveau sport.

Je suis sûr que par sa lecture un grand nombre de jeunes gens seront convaincus et voudront goûter de cette merveilleuse locomotion à travers les airs, et par là vous aurez rendu un très réel service à l'aviation.

Maurice Farman

CHAPTER 1

The Would-Be Pilot

I want to fly. The question is how and where. I have just returned from abroad with a limited amount of leave of absence, and I want to do the trick as quickly as possible. If I am unable within three months to report to the War Office that I have obtained my certificate, I shall have to rejoin my station abroad. I also want to do it as cheaply as possible, for I have had to pay my passage home, and shall also have to pay for that of my successor out. The advertisements of the various aerodromes in the aeronautical journals seem to offer all that one can reasonably demand. The general quotation seems to be for £75, which includes risks to machine and third party. I inquire the cost of insuring myself against accident and death, and receive a quotation of £15 *per cent*. This is not good enough, so I decide to risk it.

I had written while abroad to some of the best-known schools for particulars, and I found the answers awaiting me at home. Some of these were business-like, with printed forms of agreement, others of the chatty description. On inquiry at the War Office I was told that no advice was given as to what school I should go, or on what machine I should learn, except that the biplane at present was preferred to the monoplane. I had simply to get my certificate in any way I liked, and the War Office would refund me £75.

I happened to have a friend who had been flying now for a couple of years, and had a pretty thorough acquaintance with the flying business both in England and France. He advised me to go straight to the latter country, telling me I should save time, get better experience, and that the prestige of the French certificate was higher than the English one. I decided to act on this advice, and have no cause to regret that I did so. At the same time, I cannot say I should not have done as well had I stayed in England, nor would my present very limited experience justify a critical comparison on my part between the schools generally of the two countries.

Within a week of arriving home I left for Paris. I went to what was described to me as a comfortable little hotel, and which I hoped would be inexpensive. I found myself in a palace, the very atmosphere of which smelt expensive, and proved to be so. Next morning I braced myself for a struggle with the Paris telephone system, and after a series of desperate bouts I got through to the Maison Farman at Billancourt, and arranged for an interview with one of the brothers Farman in the afternoon. A long ride in the still-existing, absurdly antiquated-looking steam tram took me from the Place de la Concorde to Billancourt, and I took a seat outside the Farman Office about 3 p.m.

Sometime after 4 Mr. Dick Farman arrived, and I arranged in a few minutes for taking my brevet for £75. Even in that short time we were interrupted by the arrival of several visitors on pressing business. One of them was the minister for one of the Balkan States, and desired to expedite an order for aeroplanes for the seat of war. I was then kindly taken round the very fine new workshops by Mr. Farman, who explained some of the interesting processes in the construction of the Henry and Maurice Farman biplanes. It was interesting to see how these two brothers continued to develop their particular creations on their own lines in the same shops. The shops were humming with activity, and gave one the impression of immense human beehives.

About one aeroplane a day was being turned out, which was insufficient to keep pace with the demands. I tried to find out which of the two types of machine was in greater demand, and gathered it was about the same for both. I had to choose which type of machine I would learn on, and the difference between the two is considerable. During the last French manoeuvres *escadrilles* of both kinds had been employed. I knew that machines of both types had been supplied to the home government, but I believed that the majority were Maurice Farmans, and I knew also that a company had been started in England for the building of the Maurice machines. I decided to learn on the Maurice, which has the attractive reputation of being the easiest and safest for the beginner. Mr. Farman told me there was a school at Buc and another at Étampes, to either of which I could go, and that there was little to choose between them. For the school at Buc one would live at Versailles which was handy for Paris, while Étampes was an hour away by rail.

It struck me at once that the proximity of the Boulevards to Buc might prove a fatal attraction, so I elected for Étampes, which was said to be a better ground if anything. There was, moreover, an English officer at the latter school.

CHAPTER 2

Arrival at the School

1st day.—I arrived next day at Êtampes at the Hôtel du Grand Courrier, where Lieut. X, the English officer referred to above, was staying, and obtained an excellent room at 4 *francs* a day. The charges for meals were *petit déjeuner*, 75 *c.*; *déjeuner*, 3 *fr.*; *dîner*, 3 *fr.* 50 *c.* The *cuisine* was always excellent.

After *déjeuner* the school car started for the flying ground, which is about four miles out of the town. The *camion* would take about a dozen passengers, and on this occasion there were about half that number. Two French officers in uniform were of the party. They had obtained the ordinary certificate, or *brevet civil*, some time before, and were now training for the "*brevet militaire*" which is a very superior affair. Lieut. X was ready to take his certificate at the first suitable opportunity. He could have done so before, but was advised to hold on for a time in order to obtain further practice in the *vol plané* and flying generally. At this school, he told me, one is not hurried, nor pressed to attempt the necessary flights for one's certificate before one feels confident.

The school consists of a dozen large hangars, containing Henry and Maurice Farman biplanes. The ground is bordered on one side by the main route to Orléans, on the other by a narrow belt of trees about five hundred yards long and five hundred yards away. For the rest, the surrounding country is open and undulating, grass and stubble alternating with ploughed land, save for the relief of a number of small woods sparsely scattered. The square half mile or so of flying ground proper consists of good turf, but one can fly over the adjoining country, which is destitute of hedges or fences of any description. The narrow belt of trees mentioned above is used as the long axis of the oval followed in making a circuit, which is always carried out left-handed. The reason for always going left-handed is no doubt because some machines with rotary engines turn to the left more easily than to the right. It is an offence to make a right-handed circuit, unless there is no possibility of any other machine being about with which one might collide.

There was a certain amount of wind, and the manager and chief pilot (in this case the only pilot-instructor) proceeded to take out a Maurice and Henry machine respectively, and try the air. *Remous*, or eddies were reported, unsuited to the training of the young idea, so there was nothing to be done but watch the flights of the "old birds." One could not but be struck by the confident ease with which the old birds take to flight. A comprehensive *coup d'œil* and they climb into their seats and give the word to start up. A mechanic depresses the needle of the carburettor, places the two-bladed walnut wood propeller in a horizontal position, gives it one swing down and darts back and then out to the side clear of the tail.

Two other blue-clad mechanics meanwhile hold the machine while the pilot listens intently to the telltale hum of the engine and tries the engine control. The pilot raises his hand and the mechanics stand clear. The machine moves off, slowly at first, and then with rapidly increasing speed, rolling easily on its pneumatic-tyred wheels over the smooth ground. The tail rises clear of the ground with the blast from the propeller, the machine gradually, gets more and more on tip-toe, and leaves the earth with a very gradual rise. A few circuits are made, each buffet of wind seems to be counteracted, and any tendency to tip to one side nipped in the bud. The landings are so beautifully made that it is hard to see when contact is really made. The pilots are indeed admirable, but I returned with the reflection that in their more humble way, the mechanics upon whom the engines depend may be equally worthy of admiration.

CHAPTER 3

A First Flight

2nd day.—This was a Sunday, on which day the school was generally closed; owing, however, to the fact that Lieut. X wished to fly off his trials, the school was opened in the afternoon, and a "*commissaire*" an official of the Areo Club de France, was in attendance to witness the trials. Maurice and Henry Farman machines were taken out for trial spins by the manager and the pilot, who reported the presence of *remous* in some numbers. The decision was against Lieut. X flying for his certificate that day, but otherwise the normal work of the school was to proceed. The French officers and non-commissioned officers in waiting for the *brevet militaire* took out their Henry Farmans, and I was told to take my seat behind the pilot in the Maurice. I turned my cap round so that the peak was over the nape of my neck, and climbed up into my place.

The Maurice is provided with a double control, which permits the pupil to grasp a pair of handles on the control bar by putting his arms under those of the pilot from behind. There is also a second pair of footrests working the rudders. I am not permitted on this occasion, however, to touch the controls. I am merely to watch the pilot and see what it feels like. Well, off we go—straight into the wind. We run more and more smoothly, and I am uncertain as to when we leave the ground. We skim along near the ground, rising very gently. Suddenly we shoot up a steep hill in the air. I wonder if it is all right—we seem to be climbing so rapidly. Then we flatten out and go horizontally for a hundred yards or so; then another shoot up, and another later on, which makes one's heart jump into one's mouth at first. The rush and press of air are terrific.

My chest seems to be getting stoved in and my ribs feel inclined to give way. I have difficulty in exhaling. The smallest opening of the nasal valve seems to give too much air. My blood rapidly becomes super-oxygenated, and I experience a feeling of exhilaration. I should like to shout, or at least say, *ha! ha!* but the pressure of the wind is too great for me to say anything, and I feel it best to keep my mouth shut. My left pedal has sunk—the pilot must have pressed down his. I look over his left shoulder and see that it is so. We ought to be going round to the left. I look over the edge of the fuselage and see we are going round rapidly. What a distance we have come in those few moments! We seem to be about a mile beyond the end of the wood which we are encircling. But as I look we are getting quite close to it.

Coming along with the wind we do not travel nearly so steadily. The control is working most of the time. We tip sometimes to one side and sometimes to the other, with now and then a sudden drop or rise, but none of them alarming. The drops give one a particularly pleasant sensation of the switch-back order, but more delightful because they are so springy. The pilot motions me to look over the edge and look about generally over the ground. He evidently wishes to see if I can stand looking down at the ground which is rushing wildly past below us, and whether I am at my ease. I nod and smile to him and manage to convey the desired impression, hiding my bursting chest in my bosom.

To the quondam balloonist the conditions do not seem so strange. But now we are going down. We take a dive which felt steep at first, but then we flattened out. Now we are diving again, and it seems as if nothing could prevent the machine burying her nose in the earth. An almost imperceptible movement of the front stabilisator causes us to run parallel with the surface. Are we on the ground or are we not? I crane over the edge, but cannot quite see the wheels. Anyhow, we are slowing up rapidly, and the engine has been cut off. We are certainly on the ground and standing still—all safe. I thank the pilot (in Dutch), and scramble down, rather breathless but happy.

PUPIL SEATED BEHIND PILOT, AND HOLDING THE SECONDARY PAIR OF HANDLES

CHAPTER 4

I am Allowed to Touch

3rd day.—We started at 6.30 a.m. in the school motor from the corner of the street, the *rendez-vous* for all who required to be taken up to the school. The drive of seven kilometres was desperately cold at that early hour—just after dawn. The pilots tried the air and decided that it was not for us. I felt rather disappointed, but found consolation in my goloshes, which afforded one some comfort while standing about on the damp clayey ground. The Britishers, I found, invariably wore goloshes, while the Frenchmen seemed content to paddle about in thin pointed boots of the consistency of paper. There was nothing to do but hang about and gaze at the sky, and then turn round and glare at the flag flying stiffly on the roof of one of the hangars.

The longer one looked at the anemometer on the roof of the office, the faster it seemed to buzz round and round. Occasionally one went into a sort of waiting room provided for the pupils, and warmed oneself at the stove. The attendance this morning was not in full force—a look out of the bedroom window at 6 o'clock had evidently been enough for some. Time went on slowly till about ten or half-past, when we motored back.

At the afternoon attendance things were more hopeful, and flying started towards evening. The pupils were taken out in strict rotation, according to the order in which they joined the school. I got up in my turn and sat behind the pilot as before. The pilot pointed to my cap, which I had forgotten to turn round. The danger of one's cap flying off is a very serious one. It is almost certain to be struck by a propeller blade as it flies backward. A piece is broken out of the propeller blade which then becomes unbalanced. After that the propeller either breaks up altogether—practically explodes—or continues to whirl round, as long as the engine is running, in a lop-sided manner, bringing a frightful strain on the seating of the engine in the fuselage, eventually tearing the engine out of its place, and causing a catastrophe. I shamefacedly put my cap to rights and pulled it well down.

This time I was to hold the control bar by the second pair of handles provided for the pupil, and plant my feet on the secondary pair of pedals. We were off in a few moments. I found that I did not feel the rush of air nearly so much, nor have I subsequently felt any distress from it—at least, not in a biplane.

As soon as we were fairly going, I experienced a pleasing sense of security as though borne on a cushion of air, as if all the air between me and the earth were in the nature of a spring mattress.

We made a circuit, and landed without the suspicion of a bump. Opening the throttle while still running along the ground, we soon left the earth again for a second round. We had been flying low up to now, and desirous of not letting the pilot feel that I wished to hug the earth, I pulled the control ever so slightly back. I thought that the pilot would scarcely notice it, but I was wrong. He warned me afterwards that if I pulled the control back we should go up, lose speed, and drop sideways or on our tail. I certainly had not meant to do all that at once, but I said nothing, and decided to put no pressure on the control in any way next time.

My turn soon came round again, and I went for another couple of circuits, keeping a satisfactory contact on the controls.

Lieut. X tried a circuit and figure of eight to see if he would take the opportunity of going for his *brevet*. He flew successfully and landed nicely, but considered that there was a trifle more wind than he cared about for examination purposes, and decided to wait. He had been declared fit to take his *brevet* a week before, but wished to profit by a little more practice before leaving the school. He now wished to finish with it, but was not taking any unnecessary chances—wise man.

We were finished for the day. The normal dose, I gathered, was a couple of lessons morning and evening of two or three circuits each.

CHAPTER 5

Blank Days

4th, 5th, and 6th days.—For the next three days there was absolutely nothing to be done—literally nothing. This is excessively trying at first, especially when one is particularly anxious to get on with the job; but in learning to fly one at the same time learns patience. If I ever asked a perfect loafer, engaged in the pursuit of his trade, what he was doing, and he answered " learning to fly," I should consider there was a good deal of truth in it.

The trouble commenced with a south wind, bringing the rain. In the intervals when the rain ceased the wind usually blew harder. Most of us went religiously up to the school twice a day, and passed the painful hours kicking our heels in the waiting-room. My efforts to make up a four at bridge met with a lamentable want of success. It was considered quite an English game which they could not be expected to know. I thanked my stars I could speak French, which was the common medium of the polyglot group assembled round the stove. This was the first time in my life I had really found it useful. Even here it was not really necessary in order to learn to drive an aeroplane under the instruction of a French pilot.

This may sound strange at first, but the movements of control are learnt by holding the secondary handles of the control bar, while during flight the greatest linguist in the world would be inaudible in the roar of the engine. It was, of course, of assistance to clearly understand any instructions given by the pilot before the commencement of a flight, and his criticisms or explanations afterwards.

The military element in the party consisted of two French officers, two non-commissioned officers, two ex-non-commissioned officers (who wished to re-enter the army as officer-aviators), and two British officers. The civilian element consisted of a Frenchman, a Dutchman, a Swiss, and a German. The Swiss was afflicted with a stiff leg which necessitated his sitting up on a sack of shavings to enable him to get his right foot on the controlling pedal. Later on when this unfortunate individual tried to settle himself in the front seat of the aeroplane, he found he could not manage it at all. Nothing daunted he went successively to the Blériot and the Deperdussin schools and tried to wedge himself into their respective machines, but had finally to give it up as a bad job.

It was astonishing at first to note the intimate terms on which French officers and N.C.O.s are with each other—the same handshakings and salutations, an equal place in the social circle and in the general conversation. The possibility for this must be looked for in a high general level of education and good breeding throughout the country, In the afternoon the officers sometimes brought their ladies to join the party. The fund of small talk on these occasions seemed absolutely inexhaustible, though occasionally one nearly had a back somersault at the turn taken by the conversation, a turn which an Englishman would studiously avoid in the society of ladies. The only people flying the Henry Farmans were those in training for the *brevet mllitaire*, while all the new pupils during the whole time I was at the school came to learn on the Maurice Farman. The school was originally a Henry Farman school, and had only recently become a combined one.

By the time I left popular favour seemed to have swung round to the Maurice machine. Several of the older fliers in the party considered that the Henry was perhaps the most difficult machine of all to learn. It certainly was a matter of several months' training between the time that the Henry pilots took their *brevet civil*, and the time of their carrying out the tests for their *brevet militaire*. There is, of course, a very considerable difference in the value of the two *brevets*. Until one has obtained one's own *brevet*, it is difficult to realize how little the ordinary one means, and how much remains to be done before one is even a reasonably safe pilot for an ordinary cross-country journey.

It may be interesting to compare the tests for the two *brevets* as at present laid down, for they have been changed in the past, and probably will be changed from time to time in the future, always in the direction of making them more exacting.

The ordinary certificate is that laid down by the *Fédération Aéronautique Internationale*, and the Aero Clubs of different countries belonging to this association appoint officials to see that the tests are strictly carried out. The tests consist of two flights of at least 5 kilometres each, and an altitude flight of at least 50 metres. The course to be taken for each of the distance flights consists of a series of "figures of eight" round two posts not more than 500 metres apart. The exact shape of the figures of eight is a matter of taste or luck. Some of the figures of eight I have seen taken round these posts partook more of the nature of cross-country flights over the surrounding country, especially in a strong wind.

The altitude flight can be combined with one of the distance flights, and this is usually done to save time. Landings must be "normal"—not of the "pancake" order—and after each distance flight the machine must be brought to rest within 50 metres of a previously-indicated point, the engine being cut off not later than the moment of first touching the ground. The above tests have been carried out by a few brilliant individuals after some three days' instruction, but the average time may be put down as six weeks for those who wish to get a reasonable amount of practice in addition to passing the bare tests. It will be seen, therefore, that the ordinary *brevet* amounts to little more than a certificate to the effect that the holder is in a position to commence his more serious training as a pilot.

The *brevet militaire* is that of a fully qualified pilot, and the following are the tests which usually require four or five months' training in the French army. A cross-country flight of about 150 kilometers without landing, and a return in like manner either on the same or a subsequent day. Secondly, a triangular cross-country flight of at least 200 kilometres, with landings under supervision at each corner of the triangle. Thirdly, an altitude test of not less than 800 metres for at least three-quarters of an hour. Fourthly, an oral examination on aero-motors and internal combustion engines generally; construction of aircraft; theory of flight; map-reading and meteorology.

The special certificate of the Royal Aero Club of the United Kingdom is of a similar order but less searching.

All the French military pilots have obtained their *brevet militaire*. Only two English officers at present hold a special certificate. It is devoutly to be hoped that English officers will be given the opportunity of attaining the high standard possessed by their French *confrères*.

CHAPTER 6

I Take Charge

7th day.—There was a touch of north in the westerly wind, and flying conditions were favourable. I took my turn behind the pilot, and as we followed our usual circuit it seemed to me that I had personally more effect on the control than before. In fact I seemed to have gradually and unconsciously taken charge. I looked over the pilot's shoulder and saw that as a matter of fact he had taken his hands off the control, and was holding them out in front of him. This was extremely gratifying, and I braced myself to do my best. I moved the control in accordance with the movements indicated by the pilot's hands, which he continued to hold out in front of him. After rounding the wood he took my left hand off the control and put it on the throttle lever. We depressed the elevator and commenced to descend, and then partly throttled down.

When at a few metres from the ground we closed the throttle by pushing the lever forward to its full extent, and the noise of the engine instantly ceased. By drawing the control slightly back the elevator was brought to a horizontal position, and we glided along about a couple of feet from the ground, as near as I could judge. We lost weigh, and sank gradually, taking the earth without shock, and came to a stop about 20 yards further on, thus effecting a successful *atterrissage*. The business was over for the morning. In the afternoon I was given the front seat in which one has more control, especially over the steering pedals. I felt somewhat elated and nearly forgot to turn my cap round.

This point about the cap is certainly a great danger, and in order to obviate it I decided I had better get a helmet such as is *de rigueur* with French military men when flying. This would in any case be a reasonable measure of precaution, as safety helmets have already saved

A Left-Handed Turn With Plenty of Bank

several lives.

On the word "*contact*" given by the pilot the mechanic launched the Chauvière "*Intégrale*" propeller, and the trusty Renault engine started at the first swing. I pushed the throttle lever down so as to retard the engine; the propeller speed under these circumstances is insufficient to move the aeroplane and the mechanic can get out of the way of the tail by passing under the tail booms. I put up my hand as a sign to all and sundry to stand clear, and opened up full. We left the earth after a run of about 60 yards and moved along a few feet above the earth. I drew the control slightly towards me, and we rose rapidly. I then moved horizontally again to ensure not losing speed. One more step up like this and we were at a height of about 80 feet, which was sufficient for the time being.

We swung round left-handed and the machine "banked" up to the right. This was corrected by depressing the control to the right, which sends the right-hand ailerons up and the left ones down, and brings the machine to an even keel. It was better, I understood, to let the machine bank to some extent on the turns, as it thus turns more rapidly. Sometimes the machine fails to bank itself naturally when turning; one can then help it by giving it an artificial bank by depressing the control to whichever side one is turning. The working of the control for lateral stability is a perfectly "natural" one, *i.e.* one cannot help doing the right thing instinctively. It is just as if one had the two wings of the machine under one's two hands; if the right wing comes up too much, one just pushes it firmly down again with one's right hand, and similarly for the left wing.

The flight was uneventful, as the pilot took charge to effect the landing on the conclusion at the first circuit, and again when finally landing after the second circuit. I judged therefore that the landing was a more delicate affair than the other matters, and this indeed I found to be the case later on, in fact more so than all the rest put together.

Lieut. X then took the machine, and after a trial circuit went out for his *brevet*. He circled around the two posts alternately, making up the necessary number of figures of eight (*i.e.* five in this case, the posts being 500 metres apart), and then had to make his descent. Two men with flags stood about 100 yards from the point near which he had to stop, and about 100 yards apart. If the aeroplane was steered midway between the two men, and the engine cut off at the same time, the landing would probably be successful. Lieut. X. seemed to me to hold on rather long both as regards coming down and cutting off his engine.

At last he was coming down, but did not seem to be following a line at right angles to the one given by the guides. He pulled up safely, but alas! outside the circle described with a length of 50 metres as radius and the given point as centre. His machine had cut the circle; its direction, however, was not that of a diameter of the circle, but a chord to it. A puff of wind catching the tail, when the machine was slowing up on the ground, had made matters worse than they would otherwise have been, by slewing the tail in an unfortunate direction. The attempt was therefore held to have failed by the *commissaire*, the official of the Aero Club de France, who had come to witness the tests. This result was naturally disappointing to Lieut. X, but instructive to inexperienced onlookers.

CHAPTER 7

A Visit to the Salon

8th day.—Everyone at all interested in aviation, and who could possibly manage to do so, naturally went to the *Salon* to see the "Fourth Annual Exhibition of Aerial Locomotion." It was marvellous value for a *franc*. There one could see examples of all the more or less famous types of aeroplanes, aeromotors, and accessories. One was struck by the comparative absence of everything appertaining to balloons and dirigibles. The machines holding the various records could all be examined, and those with any successes to boast of presented a conspicuous list of them. The army and navy had both entered with a will into this exhibition, and among other exhibits the army showed the complete transport and accessories of a military *escadrille*.

The *escadrille* is the French aviation unit, and its personnel and material are designed with the object of keeping six aeroplanes permanently in the field. The transport besides carrying the personnel is designed to carry a generous proportion of spare parts, the field hangars, complete aeroplanes dismounted, and workshops. All vehicles are motor driven except the two wheeled *prolonges* for carrying aeroplanes, which are attached as trailers by a limber attachment to motor vehicles. The complete transport, set forth in military array as for an inspection, consisted of three motor cars and two motor bicycles (for intercommunication purposes), six heavy cars each drawing a two-wheeled *prolonge*, and two travelling workshops.

One of the latter was shown at work with drills, lathe, etc., worked by motors obtaining their power from a dynamo worked by the engine driving the vehicle. An enormous amount of money and labour must have been expended in the production of this excellent organisation, which stood the test of the last manoeuvres so well. Four *escadrilles* were employed on each side in the manoeuvres with some spare aeroplanes in reserve; in all about sixty machines were in the field. Reconnaissances were carried out daily at the hours scheduled on a programme, regardless of weather, and both generals were kept accurately informed of the movements of the enemy's troops.

No serious accident was sustained by any of the pilots, although several machines were damaged more or less seriously. The active aeroplanes all assembled at the places of concentration, prior to the commencement of the manoeuvres, coming from their various centres by way of the air, and afterwards returned home in a similar manner. This is indeed a wonderful record, and one might imagine that the French would be satisfied for the time being with their present organisation and rate of progress. This is by no means the case. Throughout the country a great campaign is being carried on by individuals and societies for increasing the rate of progress in aviation, improving the material and organisation, increasing the trained personnel by passing young men through the aviation schools prior to their doing their military service, and providing landing-places with hangars all over the country, particularly in the neighbourhood of Paris and of the eastern frontier.

The balconies of the Grand Palais presented the wonderful spectacle of a number of aeroplanes bought by various provinces, societies, commercial houses, theatres, etc., and by private individuals, and presented by them to the government as a voluntary contribution in token of their sense of the importance of French aerial supremacy. This grand national effort could only be made by a nation, the whole manhood of which had passed through the ranks, and which had the enlightenment to understand the importance of this new development in warfare, to take a personal interest in it, and tax itself not only publicly but privately to attain its ends. It makes one's heart sink to think what a comparatively feeble interest is taken in aviation in England, and how much the public has to learn as to the necessity for the development of military and naval aviation.

The only British exhibits I found were the Bristol aeroplanes and a British Bréguet. The former were specially well commented on in the French papers. The French technical journals gave one very little idea, however, as to the comparative merits of various aeroplanes and engines; as each machine was described, a note was added to the effect that it was in the first rank of such machines, if not actually superior to all others.

The Maison Roold gave a useful exhibition of the clothing and equipment designed for the comfort and safety of aviators. The Roold helmet is worn a great deal in France, being compulsory for military aviators. I invested in one, which I found quite comfortable, but I have not otherwise tested its merits. Monsieur Roold showed me a letter from a French officer whose life had been saved by his helmet; he had been hit on the head by a cylinder, which had flown off a rotary engine.

A length of silk woven material, known as a *passemontagne*, and looking suspiciously like the top of a lady's stocking, is recommended for wear under the helmet. It is pulled over the head balaclava-capwise, and is certainly very warm for its small size and weight. Among the exhibits were a variety of vestments made of a kind of Japanese paper, or *papier Kami,* which is waterproof, warm, untearable, and very light. I have tried a coat and found it very good, also a pair of gloves which are worn inside the usual fur-lined ones. Paper socks to put over one's ordinary socks are also sold, but any piece of paper—tissue paper is the best—does for this. The question of keeping warm in the air is a very important and rather difficult one, especially as regards one's hands. It is very dangerous if one's hands become so cold that they have not a proper feel on the control, and accidents have occurred from this.

Most French pilots wear a neat black-leather suit, lined with camel's hair fleece, consisting of coat and trousers, worn over their ordinary kit. This is a very practical kit, and does not show the dirt. It can be got for eighty *francs* in France, but is much more expensive in England. It is a very good tip, if one thinks one will be cold, to put a newspaper under one's waistcoat. One of the models dressed up on the stand looked like a travesty of a man in armour, with his helmet, breast plate, thigh guards, and shin guards. The mannequin was sitting on an aeroplane seat, which also defended him from shocks from that quarter, being constructed on the same principles as the helmet, etc.

The machine with the most fighting aspect was a Henry Farman hydroplane, with a Hotchkiss mounted in the bow of the fuselage. The machine was floating in a miniature pond in which some innocent goldfish were swimming.

All aeroplane constructors are aiming at building machines to meet the wants of the armies and navies of the world, as these at present are the only important customers. A time will come when aeroplanes will be constructed for a variety of civilian uses, but at present ninety-nine per cent, of the output is destined directly or indirectly for military uses. It is the absolute necessity for the aeroplane in war, which is tiding the industry over this present semi-experimental stage which must precede the full development. The way in which government orders are placed may make or mar the industry. In France the difficulty has for the time being been solved by forming homogeneous *escadrilles* of the various types of proved merit.

CHAPTER 8

How Not to Do It

9th day.—On the Monday morning following my weekend visit to the *Salon* I paid a visit to Buc to view the flying-ground there, which seemed to me to be inferior to that at Étampes. The Blériot School has, however, just removed from Étampes to Buc, presumably in order to be nearer Paris. Approaching the Buc ground the R.E.P. machines and hangars were in evidence. M. Robert Esnault Pelterie has recently retired from aviation. This step was forced on him by lack of government support, in spite of a record showing many brilliant achievements in practical flights, which in his case perhaps more than in any other were the outcome of close scientific application.

Then came a long line of Farman hangars which I visited. As I had to get back to Étampes I did not stay long. Only chance taxis are to be picked up at Versailles, and I had had to take a "growler" at 10 *francs* to go to Buc and back. Travelling back in the train to Étampes from the Gare Quai d'Orsay, one passes the Juvisy flying-ground on the left, which looks very restricted. Arriving again at the Étampes ground it seemed to be an ideal place. The journey from Étampes to Orléans is a very favourite cross-country flight, as one can come down almost anywhere if the engine fails.

Proceeding to take my lesson, I tried the system of rising very gently for a considerable way, including a turn. This was extremely inadvisable, so the pilot impressed on me afterwards, as a turn takes off so much weigh that it is asking too much of the engine to rise at the same time.

Between my turns I saw the first effort of one of the fledglings at managing the machine alone. After making an uneventful circuit he evidently proposed to descend, and began to come down all right. He then cut off his engine, and at the same time the machine took a heavy list to starboard. This was corrected in time, before the wing touched the ground.

The aeroplane then continued to sail along with what weigh it had left at about 20 feet above the ground, when to our horror we saw that the machine was slowly rising instead of descending, besides wobbling from side to side. When the machine had almost come to a standstill prior to a rapid descent on to its tail, the pilot mercifully opened up the throttle, and the trusty engine, picking up immediately, saved the situation by getting flying weigh on, thus automatically raising the tail and enabling the control to act. After going round once more a safe descent was made, but instead of running straight, the machine ran round in a small circle, which looked rather dangerous and must have brought a considerable strain on the chassis. No damage was done, however.

The explanation of the first attempt to land was that, having taken his left hand off the control to cut off the engine, the pilot unconsciously bore down with his right hand, thus working the ailerons, and causing the machine to drop down on the right. While correcting this mistake, the pilot pulled the control slightly towards him, instead of pushing it forward as he should have done, on throttling down; for even when the elevator is held perfectly horizontal, the tail will drop if speed be lost. The engine would have started sooner, but that the pilot pushed the throttle lever further forward instead of drawing it back when he first realized that he must regain his flying speed. When he finally landed an unconscious pressure of the left foot on the pedal must have caused the machine to "circle left."

Thus were a whole series of errors clearly demonstrated; in fact, a very useful exposition of "how not to do it."

Lieut. X brought off his tests with flying colours, and departed for England the same day.

Just at dusk a monoplane circled down from above, and landed near the hangars. It was Gilbert in a Sommer machine. (M. Roger Sommer is another who has lately had to retire from the field of aviation through lack of support, in spite of obtaining a considerable measure of success with his machines; he has returned to his former pursuit of felt-making.) Gilbert got out, a somewhat uncouth figure, looking rather like a Michelin man in his padded overalls, and looked at his engine. The engine was quite cool and in good order. "Look at that engine," he said, "forty-one hours it has gone without having to have the slightest thing done to it not even a sparking plug!"

The engine was a "Rhône," a rotary one, similar to the "Gnôme" in general appearance. It has given remarkable results with Gilbert in his almost daily flights about the country. On this occasion he had come from Tours in an hour and 40 minutes. "Pretty cold up there," he said, pointing to the sky. We pushed his machine into one of the hangars and brought him back to the town with us in the school-car.

I read in the evening paper that Lieut. Sylvestre, whom I had seen starting out on a Blériot monoplane for his station at Belfort, near the Eastern frontier, had arrived safely the same day. The journey had taken him from 7.30 a.m. to 4.30 p.m. He had had to make two descents on the way, owing to violent storms of rain and hail. This journey was carried out in the ordinary course of duty, and such fine feats are so frequent in France that they seldom call for remark.

Chapter 9

First Flight in a Monoplane

10th day.—It seemed particularly cold at the school that morning. It was, in fact, freezing. I repented after my first round of having only a thin pair of gloves on, and hurried off to the vicinity of the stove. My eyes also felt the cold, so on my next round I borrowed a pair of fur gloves and tried a pair of celluloid goggles which I had bought at the low price of eighty centimes. I eventually found that, although good enough for passenger work, the curved portions of the goggles slightly distort one's vision, and this may constitute a real danger when one has to bring the machine to land oneself. Several good pilots have told me that, after trying everything, they have eventually returned to plain glass as the best and safest, although the use of glass has, of course, one obvious drawback.

M. Pierre Verrier, an artist on the M. F. biplane, always puts even his glass goggles up on his forehead before making one of his impeccable landings. Proceedings were varied by the arrival of M. Perreyon, a noted pilot, in a Blériot, from the school over the way. He and our instructor gave each other turns in their respective machines, which was a first experience for each of them on the machine of the other. We saw that Perreyon in the passenger's seat had taken control by the end of the first circuit, for the pilot proper was holding his arms out in front of him.

M. Perreyon then kindly gave each of us a turn in his speedy monoplane. The Gnôme engine was very troublesome about starting. The propeller had to be swung in one case about thirty times before the engine consented to fire. Meanwhile the pistons were from time to time liberally douched with petrol, a steady flow of which also ran from the carburettor, causing a circular patch of frost where it evaporated on the ground. The Gnôme is all right once it gets going, but requires taking down after every fifteen hours or so of running to keep it in perfect order. It can be taken down, cleaned, and mounted again very quickly, and those who use Gnôme engines which are well cared for, swear by them.

A party of three or four of us hung on to the tail each time the monoplane was ready to start. This ensured the engine getting up to full speed before a start was made, so that the tail when released lifted at once, thus saving the tail skid from unnecessary rolling work, and enabling the machine to leave the ground more quickly. The job of holding the tail is rather unpleasant, owing to the blast, which has a very strong smell of burnt and unburnt castor oil.

It came to my turn, and I struggled up into my seat alongside the pilot through a hole in the bottom of the fuselage, which is closed by a trap-door. The draught from the tractor screw was terrible, and I hastened to adjust my goggles and get my gloves on. We left the ground in about 20 yards. The machine seemed very small and bird-like compared to the biplane. It flew wonderfully steadily. There was no machine like it, Perreyon told me after, for "holding the wind," and he said it could go out in a wind which forbade the use of other monoplanes. This may be true, but most pilots can prove to you that their machines are superior to any other.

The propeller draught was very trying at first. In fact, I could hardly breathe. I tried to breathe out, but only felt like "expiring." The experience was similar to my first ride in the biplane. Raising my hand on the way round, it was suddenly blown back on to the helmet like a piece of string, through getting into the full blast of the propeller. The fine spray of vaporised castor oil was not particularly nice. I was distinctly relieved at the end of the circuit, as I had begun to feel like blowing up, through distress in not being able to breathe. I do not suppose I should have experienced this distress on my next journey, or at any rate nearly so much, judging by what I had felt on the biplane. Well—a very jolly experience when it was all over.

I cannot imagine that a machine that goes at the pace this one did can be as safe as a slower one with more wing surface; take, for instance, the question of having to land in our restricted English fields at the greater pace. At the same time the fastest machines possible are required for strategic reconnaissance, and the present ban of the War Office on monoplanes will require reconsideration. The number of monoplanes built today, (as at time of first publication), is greatly in excess of the bi-planes; both are developing equally strongly, and both will probably be required for military aviation.

It rained all the afternoon, so I stayed comfortably in my room at the hotel, and brought my diary up to date, instead of spending a gloomy afternoon in the waiting-room of the school.

CHAPTER 10

I Fly by Myself

11th day.—A thick mist, which the November sun took a couple of hours to lighten, covered the ground. After the fog had lifted I went for two very wide circuits with the pilot behind me, and I was then told I could try a small circuit or two by myself if I liked. Feeling sufficiently confident I replied that I would. With the engine throttled down, I tried the controls once more before starting: forward and backward to depress or raise the elevator; right and left for the *gauchissement* of the ailerons; right and left pedals for working rudder to right or left; backward and forward the small lever (lying close to my left hand) for opening or closing the throttle. A wire controlling the petrol supply had been duly unhooked, and was all right, and another wire controlling the supply of air to the mixture could be left as it was. There was nothing more to do, then, before starting. The pilot told me to be careful not to go too high, and not to mount while turning.

I opened up the throttle to fairly full, and soon started moving off. I turned the machine gradually while starting, so as to head it for a straight run on the circuit (I had been warned before not to turn the machine too quickly on the ground, for fear of straining the chassis). I kept the elevator horizontal until I saw that the machine had left the ground of its own accord, and then, with a thrill of exultation, headed her for the blue! After a decent rise, I went horizontally again, and then took another rise, after which I began turning to the left. I kept the elevator as horizontal as I could, but I seemed to be getting up to a good height all the same. I shot a glance to the left, and saw that the wood which I was supposed to be going round was still there. I was still at the stage when I felt as if my eyes were glued to the elevator, and that I could not afford to take them off for looking round.

There was a certain amount of wind, and I had to work the control backward and forward, right and left, a good deal. The working of the pedals had not yet become automatic with me, as I often found myself trying to work the handles round as one would the handles of a bicycle instead of working the pedals. Anyhow, I got round all right in time, as there was all space to turn in.

I saw the starting-point, and the group assembled there looked small, and far below me. One turn was completed, and on I went with my second. The air below me seemed thick and friendly; it gave me the impression it would not willingly let me down. I passed through an eddy from time to time, and the incipient dive or rear up of the machine answered readily to the control, which I worked with a firm, decided movement, without jerks. The air seemed to say, "You have only to hold the handles in a reasonable way and I won't hurt you. These little movements of mine are only to add interest to the proceedings."

The side slaps of the wind were less sudden. I felt rocked in the cradle of the air. The lateral controls rapidly damped out these rockings, in which the air seemed to say, "You see, I can blow from all directions, but if you only keep calm and do the right thing, I'll stand by you." It was now time to think of coming down. I depressed and put my left hand on the throttle, and as I descended, gradually throttled down. When a few yards from the ground, I cut off and flattened out. At least, I imagined I was going to fly horizontally for a short distance before actually alighting. Much to my horror, I perceived I was rising instead of moving horizontally. This would not do. I opened up full at once and got good weigh on again and depressed once more. When within a few feet of the ground I cut off again and flattened out just as I was touching. I made a very fast landing, but without shock I was glad to note, and then let the machine run on to a standstill.

Well, that was a good thing over. I had run a long way from the starting-point, and it took a long time for the others to walk up. I was anxious to hear what there was to be said about my flight. The pilot congratulated me, but with several restrictions. I had gone up too high in the first place. This was accounted for to a great extent by my having mounted on the turns after all. This type of machine tends to mount when turning to the left, and requires to be repressed to keep it horizontal. This I had not grasped before. Then the switch-back landing was not all it might have been. I cut off while still too high the first time, the almost invariable mistake of beginners, who see the ground coming at them at a fearsome pace, and consider—premature-

RUDDER WIRES

AILERON WIRES

THE DOUBLE-HANDED CONTROL BAR USED ON A SCHOOL MACHINE

ly—that something must be done. The second time I cut off too low. However—well out.

The feeling of responsibility on this first flight alone was the greatest tax on the nerves I have yet felt in flying, and I felt greatly relieved when it was over. I felt the absence of the pilot behind me much more than I should have expected, although latterly he had been doing little or nothing.

In the evening I had a couple of flights with the pilot behind me, and the feeling of confidence which this imparted seemed to make me do the right thing automatically.

Note.—I have talked about "cutting off" the engine by pushing the lever of the throttle valve right down; with a Renault properly adjusted, however, this does not cut the engine right off, but leaves it running just sufficiently to keep the propeller turning slowly. This is a point of the greatest value, as by throttling right down one cuts off the propeller blast, which is always obtainable, however, in a couple of seconds by opening up.

With a Gnôme engine the most widely used aero-motor of the present day which will only run at practically full speed, one has to switch the engine right off, and if one wants to keep the engine running (as, for instance, during a long *vol plané*) one has to switch on at intervals to keep the propeller turning. If one leaves it too long and the propeller stops, or is turning too slowly, the engine will not start or pick up on switching on again—Danger!

A new carburettor has been brought out by the Gnôme Company, which will permit of the engine running at a low number of revolutions, but I have not yet seen this in use. The usual form of carburettor on Gnôme engines, such as are used on the Henry Farman machines at the Étampes School, consists of a simple pipe and jet; during its passage through the pipe the stream of petrol sucked in is vaporised and mixed with air. The amount of suction required to work this simple arrangement is only obtained when the engine is running practically at full speed.

CHAPTER 11

I am Put Back

12th day.—This was a particularly fine morning for the sport, in spite of the prognostications of all the old birds the evening before, when the sun had gone down in a red setting, and even on the ground one could feel the wind getting up, while higher up the little clouds had arranged a handicap according to altitude.

I took a turn with the pilot behind me, and we finished with a figure of eight in order to land against the wind. One should always land against the wind, when there is any to speak of, both because one is steadier and because one brings up in a shorter distance owing to more rapid loss of weigh. A side wind is particularly dangerous to land in, as with diminished weigh the machine is very easily tilted on to one wing by a puff, and the effect of working the ailerons is greatly reduced—in any case, they have practically no time or space in which to act before a wing is smashed; a more or less dangerous side-strain on the chassis is also involved.

I was told I could take a turn if I liked by myself, and follow the same course, which I proceeded to do. The circuit went fairly well, and I then had to make my figure of eight. The latter was an enormous sprawling affair, covering kilometres of air-land, and not always at the same altitude, which is one of the many desiderata to be aimed at. I made a nice straight flight home for the hangars at a height of about 20 metres. The critical business of descent had now to be undertaken, with left hand on throttle valve and right hand on the control. I tried to descend gently while gradually cutting off at the same time. I came to the end of my tether in both senses more quickly than I reckoned on. I didn't like the look of it. I did not want to land at that speed, and I instinctively did not want to rise again without the engine on; so I opened up again for a slight rise, and descended again, cutting off the engine. I landed safely enough, but fast and beyond where I wanted to stop, and ran some way beyond that again—another unsatisfactory descent of the switchback order.

The pilot said this would not do—I must descend more gradually and cut off more slowly. I felt rather sick about it, but tried to comfort myself with the thought that it might have been worse. One of the four thick rubber rings, by which each axle with its pair of wheels is slung to the chassis, had gone, and I mournfully watched the interesting operation of inserting a new one. I again tried to comfort myself with the reflection that repairs were included in the sum I had paid down.

I was fairly restored to equanimity by the time I went for another tour, this time *behind* my pilot, in which position one has a very modified command over the controls. We followed the Orléans road, travelling about 100 metres high. The usual delightful avenue of trees bordered the road. I liked the look of them less in plan than from any other point of view. We circled several times above some farm buildings where the pilot had some friends, who kept his dog for him. They all came out and waved, attracted by the insistent call of the engine. We waved back to them. The farm buildings were picturesque enough, but lost most of their picturesqueness in plan, like the trees. Give me the soft plough beneath or the green fields, and I am with you in your appreciation of the beauties of the landscape.

We moved off at length from the vicinity of bricks and mortar, and flew across some small woods. These might have been pretty too, but their deep shadows seemed to glower at one. We were soon over these, though, and headed for home. Very slowly we descended and gently throttled down, skimmed along the surface and imperceptibly took the ground.

The afternoon was still good for flying, and the pupils had three lessons apiece. There were several moments of interest during the afternoon. At one time half a dozen machines were in the air at different heights—three Blériots from the establishment over the way, and three of our Farmans. Gilbert turned up, and took out the Sommer monoplane which he had left in our hangars. Rapidly mounting to about 500 metres, he made for Paris—for the Issy-les-Moulineaux ground. A new Henry Farman was brought out of its shed, and tried by Fischer. This was of the latest type, with- out front elevating plane. It had a specially large tank, to hold 390 litres of petrol. At a rate of consumption of 27 litres an hour, this would be sufficient for 14½ hours.

The duration record at time of writing is held by Fourny on a Maurice Farman—13 hours and some minutes. It was hoped that this Henry Farman with Fischer up, would beat the above record. Being a faster machine (85 kilometres to the hour, fully loaded), it was also to be expected that it would beat existing records for distance in a given time for the longer periods. Thus is the house of Farman divided against itself. The new Farman was provided with a "Rhône" motor, now on its trial in the aeronautical world, from which great things were hoped. The long supremacy of the Gnôme as the aeroplane motor *par excellence* was challenged. This new rotary engine would be mistaken by the uninitiated for a Gnôme. Its chief difference consists in having the inlet valves controlled mechanically instead of automatically. A possible drawback lies in its having exterior induction pipes for the supply of the mixture to the cylinders, and this arrangement might cause trouble in very cold weather.

CHAPTER 12

I am Promoted Again

13th day.—This was another absolutely perfect morning for aviation. The worst one could say of it was that it was rather cold. As there seemed no sign of the wind getting up, we all tacitly held on for a time, just to let things warm up generally. One of the French officers started off on a trial for his military *brevet*, on a cross-country journey to Tours. He was disqualified on his last attempt for exceeding the time-limit allowed to cover the given distance. This was due to villainous weather and engine troubles, the latter including a broken cylinder, which resulted in a damaged propeller.

We started going out in turn about 9 a.m. After a turn behind the pilot I was told to take the front seat again, and all went well. As regards control I was told that although my movements were correct, they should be carried out sooner.

I have often noticed, when sitting behind a good pilot, that he seemed to have an uncanny knowledge of what the wind was going to do, and started making the necessary correction almost before the actual arrival of the wind buffet. In explanation of this I have frequently experienced that a strong puff of wind is heralded by a much slighter one, a sort of advanced guard, and that if one exercises a good touch on the controls checking these light winds, one is doing the right thing when the real puff comes, and that one has simply to accentuate the movement one has already commenced. To obtain the best "feel," one's touch on the control should be neither too light nor too hard, much the same as in driving a car.

I was also told again that my landings were not gradual enough. I knew I should descend gently, with engine on, to about two metres above the ground, and then cut off and flatten out, and gradually take the earth, but I had not yet got the knack.

In the afternoon I had another couple of circuits and landings with the pilot, and was then told to carry on solo. I started off, and overtook a covey of partridges, which I chased and passed over; got round the wood in no time, and pulled myself together for the landing. I descended gradually on my last turn, saw that I was truly horizontal and in the straight for the starting-point, continued descending, and cut off the engine at two metres. My idea was now to bring off this much-desired gradual contact, but—*wump!*— that was a nasty bump! I bounded up a couple of yards, but tickled her down by a series of quick depressions of the elevator, and ran out quietly. I then waited to be told off, and prepared to "take it in the neck."

It was not as bad as I expected, however: rather too high a flight; still an inclination to mount in turning; and as regards landing I *must* keep the machine going much longer, after I cut off, before touching ground. Noted for next time, but that was what I was trying to do before. I was not likely to do it worse, I reckoned, and ought to do it better. All the staff came up and shook the chassis and felt the wires. One of the latter had gone, the right one, from the front of the right skid to the boom of the lower plane. It was only a case of "*bang went saxpence*," and was rapidly renewed.

Meanwhile, the other pupils were taken on the second machine. I was then doctored up with further precautions, and started on another run. Nothing eventful occurred till the landing. Last time I had landed on an upward slope, which I had not sufficiently taken into account. I cut off at the two metres height, and kept the machine up long enough to land with only a slight bump. This was better, but not good enough, and I had landed slightly on the turn, to stop near the sheds. My mental notes were confirmed by the words of the pilot, near whom I had stopped. He told me I should have carried straight on instead of worrying about stopping near the sheds.

So I went off again, and brought off much the same sort of landing, but quite straight. I was a long way from home, so I started off on a fourth round. I took a very wide turn this time, and decided that the only thing left to try to improve matters was to keep the elevator perfectly horizontal after cutting off at two metres. I got on to the line of the straight for home in good time, descended gently, cut off at the right height, and kept her floating at that. This seemed all right—floating along nicely—"must touch soon, I suppose," was what passed through my mind. I kept the elevator just nibbling, as it were, at the horizontal, and found myself running out without having felt the ground. I hooked up the petrol wire and climbed down. I received congratulations from the pilot, who confirmed the idea of keeping the elevator horizontal after cutting off, and thus letting the machine settle down horizontally for the last two metres of height, while it lost weigh. I felt very pleased at having grasped the right idea to work at now in my landings.

One of the pupils who started a day after me, wound up the day with a couple of solo circuits with perfectly satisfactory landings.

Another week, we were told, and we should be practising for the *brevet*. This was extremely cheering.

The officers and N.C.O.s, practising on the Henry Farmans, were gradually working up to greater heights in this good weather combined with longer periods in the air, and practising *vols planés* of moderate height at first, but gradually increasing.

One of the N.C.O.s showed me

Les Dix Commandements de l'Aviateur.
1. *Ton appareil, examineras Avant de partir, soigneusement.*
2. *Tous les organes, vérifieras Bien, l'excellent fonctionnement.*
3. *Ton moteur, tu t'assureras Qu'il est en parfait rendement.*
4. *De l'atmosphère, étudieras L'état si souvent inclément.*
5. *Ton casque tu n'oublieras, Il te garantira sûrement.*
6. *Le départ enfin tu prendras, Avec sang-froid, courageusement.*
7. *Centre les éléments, lutteras, Mais n'oublie pas d'être prudent.*
8. *Ta mission tu accompliras Avec soin et très sérieusement.*
9. *Nos trois couleurs tu porteras Avec joie, partout, triomphalement.*
10. *Et pour la France sacrifieras Ta vie, s'il le faut, glorieusement.*

J. A. B.

CHAPTER 13

I Fly Ten Times Over

14th day.—Decidedly the winter seems to be the flying season *par exc*ellence, and November the best month in it in this part of the world. The perfectly still mornings characteristic of early Novembers are perfect for the sport. The slight touch of frost in ground and air this morning added a *joie de vivr*e.

After the customary minute examination of the aeroplanes and engines, the manager and pilot tried the air. All being reported well, the fledglings were permitted to try their wings. I made a circuit round the wood, and effected a landing—all right it seemed; so I opened up again, ran on and got off, and effected another circuit, landing again with fair success. There was still an unprofessional ripple about the final stage of the descent, and I could generally feel when I touched.

The next pupil then carried on. This was his second solo flight. The pupils' flights at this stage are naturally of more than ordinary interest. He went off and got round all right, but the great query is always the landing. He cut off high, and then mounted rather higher. (In taking off one's left hand to cut off, the remaining hand unaided is very apt to make some slight involuntary movement.) He depressed, however, before it was too late, and after a big ripple, landed with a slight bump or two. He evidently thought it all right, though, and was off again on his second round. He made a similar landing, and came running up very pleased. The pilot took him somewhat to task.

Flying was over for the morning, as a slight southerly wind had brought up a dense fog. Going back to the town, I took a lesson in driving the school car, from the very amiable chauffeur.

Conditions were excellent in the afternoon, and I did four circuits with landings in rapid succession.

Pupil No 2 had a couple of rounds. In his final landing he positively

A RIGHT-HANDED TURN WITH A FAIR AMOUNT OF BANK

soared up after cutting off, from which position he had to do a miniature *vol plané* down. He brought it off all right, but the danger was that, having very little weigh on, a treacherous puff might easily upset him sideways. He tried again, and this time again cut off rather too high, and then sailed along without any loss of altitude. The tail began to drop, and one wondered when he would elect to come down. The tail dropped more, but mercifully the whole machine was now settling down. The tail touched first, which immediately brought the chassis to earth with somewhat of a bump, but no apparent harm was done. Pupil No. 2 seemed rather more pleased than the occasion warranted, but he was of an eminently French sanguine temperament.

Pupil No. 3, the one who nearly slid back on his tail the other day, then went out. I knew he was nervous, as earlier in the afternoon he had said he was not going out any more that day. He seemed to me to smoke too many cigarettes, and had a *bella-donna* look in the eyes. I swung the propeller for him, usually an easy job on the stationary Renault engine, compared to the business of swinging the propeller for the rotary Gnôme. In the latter case you have to swing engine and all, and it is usually more difficult to get it to fire. This business of swinging the propeller is a frightfully dangerous looking thing at first, as the blades begin to fly round almost before the man's hands have left, and the madly whirling knives seem to be going round precious near his face.

It is, in fact, an operation in which due caution has to be employed, the great thing being to avoid slipping at the critical moment, and falling with one's head in the fatal disc. Well—No. 3 got off and disappeared behind the wood, as usual. Suddenly, the hum of his engine ceased, and did not start again. I started running for the end of the wood, and the rest followed, the school car bringing up the rear. A variety of conjectures passed through one's mind as to what might have happened, and as to what possible gruesome spectacle one might be treated. I guessed, however, allowing for the state of mind with which I credited him, that he had merely surprised himself into landing, by suddenly finding himself too low through inadvertence; that he had cut off and landed instead of rising. We ran on and round the end of the wood. . . .

Well in the open we saw the machine at rest, apparently all right, with No. 3 examining the chassis. This was a great relief. We assured ourselves that both pilot and machine *were* all right, and were then treated to a lengthy explanation, accompanied by much gesticulation:

how he had made a large circuit, and was steering in a general direction for home, when suddenly tall, dark, and menacing, the great black wood elevated itself before him. Uncertain of making good his turning round the end of this menacing obstacle, he thought it better to come down, and had effected a good landing, in spite of a number of large stones strewn about.

This was an interesting and surprising yarn. The fact was that he had completely lost his head. The machine was a good hundred yards from the wood, and the track of the wheels extended nearly another fifty yards back, and in a direction which showed that the descent had been made not towards the wood, at all, but in the correct direction for home. There was sufficient room to have made a complete circle without touching the wood or even going dangerously near it; the said wood was only a narrow copse of small firs, and a slight draw on the lever must of a certainty have carried him safely over.

The pilot then took up No. 3 as a passenger, just to show him how he *could* turn, and got badly caught in the eddy of his own tail—rather a new experience for the pilot, I fancy.

I made four more circuits, landing each time, and taking a greater height during flight. On one occasion, after landing and running along on the wheels, I hooked up the petrol wire, with a view to stopping the engine and getting out; on looking up after this momentary diversion, I found to my horror that I was floating up in the air again! I had got more weigh on than I realized, and had unwittingly drawn back the control somewhat. I depressed immediately and landed gently. As the propeller was still moving I released the petrol wire, and opened up again just to show I could do better. The final landing really seemed all right, and the pilot complimented me. When coming down from these greater heights, he said, it was certainly best to throttle down a good deal, on account of the added velocity from the descent.

I hoped I had now got hold of the right ideas to aim at in landing. My idea now was to flatten out at two metres high, and then keep the machine—*not necessarily the elevator*—horizontal, until she dropped of her own accord to earth. One then landed on the four wheels, and the tail dropped gently afterwards.

CHAPTER 14

Ready for the Brevet

Sunday.—The chance of a last visit to the *Salon* was not to be missed. I had a good look round from 9 to 11 a.m., after which the place began to get crowded. I paid another visit in the afternoon, and was occasionally carried off my feet by the crowd. The national enthusiasm over aviation was most remarkable, and reached its maximum when the band played "*La Marseillaise des Aviateurs.*" It is the military aspect of aviation, with the hope of the success it will bring them in their next war, which makes the chief appeal to the people, and the success of the show was due in great part to the active co-operation of the fighting services. The number of types of hydroplanes exhibited was another remarkable feature. This branch of aviation is advancing with giant strides. The absence of Paulhan with his "Triad" was noticeable, due it was said to the impossibility of sparing a single machine of the type even for a fortnight.

15th and 16th days.—*Monday and Tuesday.*—Wind, rain, fog, etc.—nothing doing. I occasionally got into the seat of a Maurice, and worked the control and my imagination in unison.

17th day.—*Wednesday.*—Not too bad. The pilot told me to start quick before the wind got up. So I pushed off and did four circuits with landings, all going very well. I was just beginning to make the necessary movements automatically, including the steering with one's feet, which at first seemed unnatural.

The pilot said I could go for my *brevet* when I liked.

A thick fog came up directly I had finished, and closed proceedings for the day. I drove the school car back under instruction, and up and down again in the afternoon. Fog prevented any further flying.

18th day.—*Thursday.*—Nothing doing again. This was very dull. I wandered about in the workshops, and tried to get some instruction about the engines. Some of the school prospectuses in England contain clauses as to instruction being given in the care and repairing of engines, etc., but there is not as a rule much organisation about this part of the teaching; nor is this difficult to understand, as much attention paid to this portion of the business would prove a costly and unprofitable undertaking. It would in any case be hard to arrange and carry out, as the knowledge of the pupils on the subject varies between such wide limits. While few of them are entirely ignorant, many are experts. In any case there is no examination on aero-motors for the ordinary certificate, such as there is for the French *brevet militaire*, and the expense of instruction in this subject would be a loss to competitive schools catering to pass candidates simply through the tests for the certificate at so much a head. The minimum that is required to be known is soon picked up, however, together with the leading features and characteristics of the engines with which one has to do.

The two most commonly used engines in the motor world are the Gnôme and Renault, and their chief points may be summarised as under

Gnôme.—This is a radial engine of the rotary type, with seven cylinders. The types on the market are of 50, 70, 80, 100, 140, and 160 horse-power. The last three consist of two of the corresponding lower powered ones worked together on one shaft, the cylinders of the back unit showing through the spaces between those of the one in front.

The cylinders are of steel, and very thin, and are made with fins to facilitate air-cooling, which is also greatly aided by the revolution of the engine itself. In practice it is a very reliable engine, and is generally regarded as a marvel of skilled design by the engineering world. It requires, however, much attention and specially trained mechanics to look after it properly. To keep it in perfect order it has to be taken down after about thirty hours' running, cleaned, and re-erected. This takes two skilled mechanics a ten-hour day. The reason for this constant cleaning arises from the free deposit of carbon in the cylinders from the burnt oil.

The propeller is fixed to a boss on either the front or back plate of the crank-case, and thus revolves at the same number of revolutions as the engine, *i.e.* at about 1200 revolutions per minute.

One of the great features of the engine is the ease with which it can be mounted on any machine, which in a great measure accounts for the general manner in which it has been adopted for many different types of machines. There is an objection from a certain number of people to the use of this engine, in common with other rotary engines, on account of its gyroscopic action. The effect of the gyroscopic action may be slightly felt when making a turn to the right.

It is very wasteful both in oil and petrol. The weight of a 50 horse-power engine is only 150 lb., or 3 lb. per horse, and it is this wonderful lightness which is its greatest advantage. When one sees one of these engines starting, and the light frail-looking working parts beginning their mad dance, one imagines that the whole thing must fly to bits with the centrifugal force developed.

The price of a 50 h.p. is £400.

Renault.—This engine is very similar to the well-known car type except that it is air-cooled instead of being water-cooled. A revolving fan in front of the engine drives air past the cylinders, while aluminium shields direct a part of this current upwards between the cylinders. It is a stationary engine of eight or sixteen cylinders, set V- shaped.

The types on the market are of 50, 70, and 100 h.p., of 8, 8, and 16 cylinders respectively.

The cylinders are of cast iron, and likewise the cylinder heads; both of which, and the top of the sparking plug, have fins to facilitate the air-cooling.

It is a very reliable engine, and requires comparatively little attention. The accessibility of the working parts leaves much to be desired, but the engine does not often require taking down—say, every 60 hours. The cylinder heads can be removed, and the cylinders cleaned, valves ground, and can all be put back by a mechanic in half a day. If the whole engine has to be taken down, it is a heavy job, and it is awkward to get it out of the nacelle. It would take two good mechanics, with assistance in lifting the engine, three days to take down, clean, and re-erect.

The propeller is fixed to the end of the cam-shaft, and revolves at 900 revolutions to the engine's 1800, the cam-shaft being geared down from the crank-shaft at 2 to 1. A larger measure of efficiency is obtained from the larger propeller travelling at a slower speed, than from a smaller high-speed propeller; the amount of gyroscopic action is negligible.

A 70 h.p. Renault uses 7 gallons of petrol an hour, and ¾ of a gallon of oil. It weighs 430 lb., or $6^{1./7}$ lb. per horse.

The price of a 70 h.p. Renault is £480.

From the manager I tried to get some notes as to the administration of such a school as this, and received many polite promises.

From the clerk I obtained a record of my flying time up to date, which was as follows:

Flying days.	Minutes.
1st	41 with pilot.
2nd	11 " "
3rd	6 " "
4th	15 " "
4th	23 alone.
5th	65 "
6th	65 "
7th	50 "
8th	23 "

Total—5 hours all but a minute.

The above times were made up of several short flights, as a rule, and were generous estimates, I should say, probably to make sure of accounting for all the petrol used.

It was still raining, and feeling very bored I walked back to the hotel. The first five kilometres were fairly pleasant walking, along a decent road; but the last two kilometres through the town were killing, the paving consisting of very rough stone, about 6-inch cube, very uneven and full of holes. A mile or two over this tires one out, and one arrives at one's destination feeling jarred all over. One hears much of the fine roads of France, but in our small towns the roads are infinitely better than this. The effect of this sort of road, which extends for miles from Paris in some directions, must be nothing less than disastrous to the bolts and springs of cars.

CHAPTER 15

Final Practices for the Brevet

19th day.—The afternoon proving favourable, I was told I could have the machine, and do more or less what I liked with it. So I started off and tried some figures of eight round a couple of imaginary points. I found I was carried about half a mile to leeward while I was on the turn, which made my figures rather shapeless. I had got over the inclination to mount on the turns, and was now rather the other way, which was preferable. The pilot told me I would do better to work at a higher altitude, so as to allow for sinking on the turns.

So the next time I got up to rather over 50 metres, which is the height to be attained in the altitude test for the *brevet,* and passed over the wood while making the "eights," instead of going round it each time. This made the figures more stylish. The landing (against the wind) was in each case imperceptible, so I felt pretty confident for the tests, which specify "normal" landings. One of the pupils who was carrying out his tests just before I joined, landed in the middle of the given circle very exactly, but the landing was unfortunately of the pancake variety, and broke up the chassis.

The time-keeper, who swore to his exactitude, had noted the duration of my two flights as 10 and 12 minutes respectively. The latter would be my longest non-stop solo flight to date. I felt I could easily carry on for an hour. This would carry me 85 kilometres, with an expenditure of 30 litres of petrol. I should certainly have liked to fly for an hour, in order to say or rather to feel I had done it.

The French officers and N.C.O.s were in fact training until they could do an hour at 500 metres altitude. This done, they would join one of the military aviation centres, and undergo further training for the military *brevet.*

20th day.—Saturday. Rained all day.

21st day.—Monday afternoon was perfect for flying—not a breath of wind. The first time I got hold of the machine I did my five "figures of eight" round two imaginary points, at a height of about 50 metres, passing over the wood as required, so as not to spoil the symmetry of the figures.

I made an attempt to land in the circle marked on the ground as the usual stopping-place for the trials. I did not, however, see the spot in time, with the consequence that I ran over the circle after landing. But as there would be a flag or something to mark the spot on the day of trial, this failure did not worry me much.

It was some time before I could get hold of the machine again, as there were two other pupils now flying alone.

A bran-new one also turned up, accompanied by his parents. The new-comer was given a passenger flight, "with which he declared himself enchanted," according to the almost invariable formula in the aviation journals the day following a new "baptism of the air." The new chum's father was also taken for a turn, and was previously over-heard to say that he must have a flight to see if his legs got cold, and whether it would be really necessary to get Marcel leather trousers as well as coat. (As he had only a short trip, and it was a warm day, pater-familias's legs did not get cold, and the son never got his trousers.)

Madame, meanwhile, was making inquiries as to whether her boy would find himself in a "*bon milieu*" and looked the rest of us up and down in a very searching manner.

When I got the machine again I noticed there was an aneroid attached to the front of the fuselage, so I determined to have a little altitude trial all to myself. I only needed to get up to 50 metres for the trial, so I opened up full and headed for the blue-grey. On looking at the aneroid for the first time after starting I saw I was already at 75, so I said "Good enough," and rung round the wood, making a gradual descent, and landed, or rather stopped, inside the circle.

I felt I could easily work at a higher altitude if necessary, so I was satisfied for the present.

There was no further time that day to fly off the trials, which would take from half an hour to an hour, but I was told that if it was fine the next day, as seemed probable, I could carry them out. One of the French officers would be willing to act as *commissaire*.

At this stage the inevitable photographer, who took all the pupils

THE TAIL SHOULD BE WELL UP AND FLYING SPEED ATTAINED BEFORE THE MACHINE IS PERMITTED TO LEAVE THE GROUND

as a matter of course, turned up. He was not to be denied, and had his will of me. Four photos are required in any case nowadays to accompany the application for the *brevet*, and the pupils at the French schools do a good deal in the way of exchanging photos in the form of postcards.

CHAPTER 16

The Brevet

22nd day.—The morn bid fair, and after turns taken by the pilot and two other pupils, I started off to do the necessary for the *brevet*. The pilot's final injunction was to roll well before rising from the ground, so as to make sure of having due weigh on, and avoid rising with a drooping tail, which would be thoroughly bad style. I determined to do nothing so amateurish. I was provided with an aneroid slung in front of me, which I could read easily, and a pocket barograph, a very neat little instrument, lent to me by one of the pupils, the Dutchman. I decided to fly at about 100 metres, that being a decent height, and not too high to prevent one easily seeing the flags, about which one had to turn. The pilot said he would wave a flag when I had done four figures of eight, so that I should then know that I had to make one more figure, and then land.

I went off and got my altitude during the first figure, trying to rise on the straights only and avoid turning on the curves. I seemed to be getting along famously, and quite forgot to look out for the signal on my fourth figure. I saw violent signs being made as I finished my fifth, but as I had rather lost count by this time, I made one more to be quite sure, and then did a circle round the wood, making altogether, as I was told afterwards, six and a half!

Two markers stood about 100 yards from the stopping point, and the thing was to steer midway between them, and at right angles to their line. This I managed to bring off all right, having made a very big sweep round, so as to get a long straight. I came along about six feet above the ground, and cut off as I passed the markers, having already throttled down to a certain extent. I ran over the centre of the circle and stopped about ten yards beyond. This was satisfactory. The pocket barograph showed a line of dots at the 100 metre level, representing my flight. This was the end of the first test.

I now proposed to go straight on, and combine the other two tests, namely a second series of five figures of eight, and the altitude test of 50 metres. For this purpose I had a sealed barograph slung in a box on my back. I still had the other in my pocket, and the large aneroid in front of me. Off I went again with instructions to look out for waving on my fifth figure, which I was to complete, and then do the altitude test—100 or 200 metres, or whatever I fancied above the 50. I completed the five figures of eight at about 100 metres without incident, having noted the waving, which I was this time on the lookout for. I then set out for altitude.

The first thing I concentrated on was to see the aneroid mark 200, without rising appreciably on the curves. I was making large circles round the wood. The 200 was so soon and easily attained, that I thought I had better make sure of good measure by going to 250. I still felt quite master of the situation, so I determined to push on with a third oval and make it 300. I now began to feel rather less sure of myself, as sometimes when I felt sure I was mounting, the aneroid did not seem to show it, and then when I felt I was going horizontally, or even slightly down, the aneroid seemed to be going up quite quickly. The instrument must have had a certain retardation, but this discordance between fact and fancy was disconcerting.

Well—I arrived at 300, and was still going round. At this height movement seemed quite slow. I could easily fancy I was not moving at all—just sitting still in a buzzing chair. Rapidly multiplying 300 by 3, and finding that this fell short of 1000 feet, I determined to make for 350, which would give a decent margin. Long clouds of fog were streaming up from the south, and frequently nearly hid the wood and the ground generally from view. But I could just see well enough to steer by. Having had my confidence slightly shaken by the unsympathetic behaviour of the aneroid, I went very gently indeed: in fact I seemed to be unable to rise at all. The low fog had obscured the horizon, and I found that the effect was that one soon lost one's sense of the horizontal under these circumstances.

Ordinarily, by seeing what the edge of the front elevator is doing with regard to the horizon, one has a sound guide. I was not sure now what I was doing, whether I was going down, horizontally, or up. The awful thought struck me that I might be going up at some impossible angle, dangerously "*cabré*," and I shot a pained glance at my aneroid, that broken reed, which I considered had failed me in the hour of necessity. It marked something slightly over 300. After all, I thought, I was pretty steady; if the aspiring aviator begins to conjure up bogies, he might as well put up the shutters. It required considerable effort, however, to pull the control now, so as to either feel like rising, or have any effect on the aneroid. I pulled resolutely, and was certain I was rising.

The aneroid started rising soon after. I determined to come down at 350, as I was beginning not to like it. I hung on like grim death, and leaning forward I saw the needle well over the 350 mark, and depressed. The wretched aneroid still continued to rise, which made me depress more, and more than depressed me, as I had not really had a calm moment in which to size up the nature of the beast. When it did begin to drop the aneroid certainly dropped very quickly, much too quickly I considered. I determined to take plenty of time about it from then on.

In about three large ovals I got down to the region of 50 metres, and then rung round the wood, and made an exactly similar landing to the previous one, *i.e.* stopping about 10 yards beyond the centre of the marked circle. I hooked up the petrol wire, undid the belt which fastened me into the seat, and began to climb down. The others called out to stop me, until the *commissaire* came up and removed the sealed barograph. I then got down and we looked at the records. The pocket barograph showed 400 metres, the official one 365, while the one I was looking at had marked 355 when I began to descend, and I had not noticed to what height it had gone exactly during the early part of my descent. The differences in reading were accounted for by the fact that the aneroid slung in front of me had been adjusted to something below zero before I started, so as to give the official instrument, a noted laggard, time to mark somewhere near the height attained. The pocket instrument was the most delicate of the three, and probably correct.

The deed having been done, all and sundry were most congratulatory. The pilot said I had been too high, but was distinctly pleased. For another he would have had fear, he said, but in this case he trusted to British phlegm.

The fog was now thick, so we dispersed. Having arranged to carry on with further training, I turned up as usual in the afternoon, and got a couple of good flights, not going much above 100 metres, but going in for steering over fresh country, steering on a distant mark, following a road or railway, etc. I also found out how warp and rudder help each other, so that in practice one gets into the way of seldom using the one without the other.

One of the other pupils flew his tests, but not in good style, as he kept very low, and only did about 70 metres for his altitude.

An instructive accident occurred to a Henry Farman on landing, as I was watching it. The officer flying the machine, who had had considerable experience, was landing gently after a *vol plané;* he had elevated slightly just before landing, so as to clear the plough at the edge of the ground, and had very little weigh on. The ground sloped up to his right, and as he kept his planes horizontal, the right wheel touched first. What happened then was that the two struts immediately above the right pair of wheels snapped in half, and the machine tipped forward, breaking off the ends of both skids. Some other minor damage was done, but as the machine did not turn over the pilot was unharmed, being luckily strapped to his seat. It seemed to me that the chassis broke rather easily, and I did not think this would have occurred with a Maurice Farman. The Henry machine in question was a 13 metre one, of a newer and lighter pattern than the older 17 metre one, and designed for greater speed. It has a distinctly more fragile appearance.

CHAPTER 17

Subsequent Practice

The time subsequently passed by me at the school I employed for cruising round the environs generally for as long as I was permitted to have the machine; this was never more than half an hour, as there was always someone else waiting for his turn. The pilot had promised to come up with me, and put me in the way of the *vol plané*. He explained that I should certainly have had some little experience of this before going anything like as high as I did when passing the *brevet*; if anything had gone wrong with the engine when in the air, I should have had to plane down. The force of this reasoning was manifest, and I was only too anxious to learn the elements of the *vol plané*, and thereby take a reasonable measure of precaution against engine mishaps in future flights.

Well, the pilot always seemed to be very busy with new pupils, who were flocking up daily, and as the manager of the school was on leave getting married, the pilot was also acting manager for the time being, and so had less time than ever. I therefore came to the conclusion that if I was going to learn this thing I had better teach myself. I had already started on a very small scale in some previous flights "*en faisant la montagne russe*" *i.e.* by switchbacking the machine, throttling down the engine while descending, and opening up again for the rise. This is quite an exhilarating form of play at first, especially combined with a rocking of the ailerons, and only advisable for a beginner on a perfectly calm day.

It is wonderful how rapidly and easily the machine will rock when the handles are quickly moved up and down, The machine answers at once, without any retardation. It acts so easily, too, that one seems to be rocking the house with one's little finger. When the machine answers like this to the lateral working of the command, one knows from that alone that the machine has got all due flying speed on—and this is a useful check in climbing, for instance, against rising too rapidly. An occasional waggle of the command should be followed by a corresponding rocking of the machine—then all is well, and you may continue to climb at that. If there is no corresponding rock, or if it is late and feeble—beware! you are losing weigh.

Having decided, then, to fathom the mysteries of the *vol plané*, as soon as I had secured the machine, I proceeded to a height of some 50 metres, and after a preliminary switchback or two, I pushed the throttle lever full down, and proceeded to descend.

Now if there is one thing about a Maurice Farman more than another which is rubbed into one *ad nauseam* in all one's reading of the comparative virtues of various machines, it is its almost uncannily low gliding angle. I said to myself therefore, "Let us take advantage of our wide and deep reading on these things. Of what use, indeed, is theoretical knowledge unless applied to practice when opportunity offers? We will proceed to glide at 1/10 or thereabouts." We seemed to be swishing along nicely, and evidently the whole art of *vol planing* seemed to me must consist in taking the smallest possible gliding angle. I was not, however, quite happy: the swishing seemed to be dying away, but go down steeper I would not.

Had not I read the whole matter up, forsooth? Of what use then were books? I could swear I was descending at about the best angle, as shown in the pictures in some of the highest authorities on the subject. All the same, things were going from bad to worse, there could be no doubt of that. The swish had quite died away, an ominous wobble was beginning to make itself felt—this without either wind or working of the *gauchissement* to account for it. I wobbled the lateral command—horrors! there was practically no response. I felt that in another moment I should be standing still, and then—but no! I felt in a fraction of a second that if I came dropping down on my tail, in a Maurice Farman too, of all machines, I should not only suffer a serious accident, but should also make myself a laughing-stock.

I decided to postpone further experiments. I shoved her nose down, I turned on the engine full blast, I got so much weigh on the old bus that I could make her rock by merely thinking of the ailerons. Flattening out to relieve the pressure on my ears, I sailed round to the back of the wood and some distance off for my next experiment. I clung tenaciously to my theory of the weirdly low gliding angle, and the proper way of putting that precious knowledge into practice.

Again and again did the machine fail to go down according to my expectations. " I'll go back and think it out," I said to myself, " especially as the other chap's waiting." It also occurred to me that I seemed to have forgotten I was now paying for damages.

I returned and strolled toward the hangars, as if I knew nothing of important experiments which had recently been conducted in the neighbourhood on the subject of aviation. My return was unmarked in any way by the sort of comments I was expecting. I had hardened my face, preparing to be told I had been making an ass of myself. At the same time I was somewhat disappointed at the entire absence of comment, and therefore proceeded to draw one of the *sous-officiers*, an experienced flier, who was standing about. After a general conversation, I casually remarked as I was leaving him that I was commencing the *vol plané*.

"Yes," he said, " but you were going too flat."

"I thought so," I lied.

On my way to my machine I passed the pilot, who was changing pupils on the other machine. "You cut off your engine before beginning to descend just now, didn't you?" he said.

"Yes, isn't that right?" I replied.

"Get your apparatus engaged at the right angle of descent first and get her going well down before you cut off."

This was enough. Armed with these instructions I got into the machine again, determined to leave fine gliding angles well alone for the present. I went up to 100 metres, put the machine well down to a useful angle of descent, and then cut off. I felt I was going at more than normal flying speed, "*vitesse de régime*," but I avoided all inclination towards a more gradual angle. I felt a strong and constant wind in my face. Keeping the nose of the machine well under, the odd simile of drowning a kitten came to me. Instead of the humming roar of the engine, I heard as we (the machine and I) descended, ever at the same angle, the constant swish of the planes; it seemed the most beautiful music I had ever heard.

Anything more beautiful than the sensation of this flight, I had never experienced. But here was mother earth. Gradually flattening out and opening up the engine, I proceeded to take height again, and went through exactly the same performance. Coming down I worked the lateral command, and the machine rocked in unison. The pedals swung her easily to right and left. Nearing the end of my tether I turned the engine on, and made a normal landing. Even after this I

A VOLPLANE AT A SAFE ANGLE OF DESCENT

was subsequently told I had been going rather flat!

On the next occasion I determined to make my landing without the engine. I proceeded as before, and having descended to about 30 feet from the ground, I flattened out gradually in an asymptotic curve, and ran her out nicely to $y = o$.

This felt really great and glorious, and I did it once more, all going well. The joy of *vol-planing* really beats anything I have ever experienced.

I was glad I had done this, as I never got the machine again. A whole week of bad weather prevented my doing further flying, and the time had come when I had to leave the school.

CHAPTER 18

Miscellaneous Notes

Average flying time required to secure a certificate. I obtained from the clerk at the School Bureau the number of flying hours taken by all the pupils on the Maurice Farman machine up to date at that school. The results were as follows:

Number of pupils.	Hours.	Minutes.
1	8	24
2	8	27
3	10	—
4	6	42
5	7	7
6	7	2
7	4	9
—	—	—
Totals 7	51	51
Average time	7	24

The average time in flying hours may, therefore, be taken as 7½ hours, of which one half to three quarters of an hour would represent the time taken in flying off the actual trials for the certificate. My own time was 7 hours and 2 minutes, number six in the above list. Number seven took only a short time, but he was inclined to be in too great a hurry to take his certificate, and was not a strong flier at the time of his passing.

As regards the number of flying days, this naturally depends on the weather. The whole business has been done in two or three days, but, as a rule, not more than half an hour's flying per day is given on the average, and more than this is not usually considered advisable at first. A good deal is learnt by being about and watching pilots and other pupils. In my case I flew on thirteen separate days out of a total period of twenty-six days including four Sundays on which the school was not open. I happened to hit a favourable period after the Balkan officers had left for the seat of war and before a number of new pupils, chiefly English officers, had begun to arrive. The weather was on the whole favourable.

After the trials are over, there is a delay of some three weeks in receiving the actual certificate. In the case of an Englishman or other foreigner getting his certificate in France there is a delay of some seven weeks while the various Aero Clubs communicate with each other.

Cost of subsequent practice.—The cost at which practice may be carried out after finishing with the certificate was quoted to me as 500 *francs* a week, or, if by flying time, at 200 *francs* an hour. The cost of remaining on at the school with a view to taking the *brevet militaire* would have been 4000 *francs*. This latter sum was said to be a special minimum for English officers, and is, like the £75 for the ordinary *brevet*, much less than is paid by the French Government to the various schools on account of military pupils. This is accounted for by the long time sometimes taken by the military pupils, and the thorough nature of the training for the *brevet militaire*, which comprises several distinct stages, namely

Vol plané from 500 metres.
Hour's flight above 500 metres.
Cross-country flying.
Examination in aero-motors.
Finally, the tests laid down for the *brevet militaire.*

Precautions.—The wearing of a safety helmet is generally conceded to be a sound precaution.

As regards strapping one's self in, there is some difference of opinion. In some cases people have probably been saved by being thrown clear, but it is much the same problem as the tight or the light-hearted hunting-seat. I fancy, if it could be compiled, that the record would favour the tight seat in an aeroplane, and the strap certainly keeps one in one's place in the event of an extra rude buffet which would otherwise throw one against the control and possibly cause a false movement.

Tips.—I have been told by an English pilot that he generally got

£5 from a pupil on the latter passing for his certificate. A similar tip is not so usually made in France, but I gathered that 100 *francs* was often given; in any case the *billet* for that amount which I tendered was gracefully accepted. Some French pilots get a sum of say 50 *francs* from their *Maison* or *patron* for each pupil passed for his certificate.

Conclusion

I trust that anything I have written in the above diary will be regarded merely as a record of experiences, and not be taken as intended for instruction. If, however, these notes should prove of interest or help to anyone about to learn to fly, I should be greatly pleased.

What would give me the greatest satisfaction would be to convey to some, who can only regard aviation as flying in the face of Providence, a more accurate idea of what is actually involved in the way of risks and difficulties, which are considerably less, for instance, than in mountain climbing; to certain others, who might be hesitating whether to take the plunge or not, I should like to give the last needed touch; to certain others, again, who have formed the impression that the certified aviator necessarily knows all about flying, I should like to say once more that he is only at the beginning of the two or three years of constant training and practice necessary to make the perfect pilot; and lastly, to all who are not already aware of it, I would point out that we are getting left in the race for aerial supremacy, and losing that position which should go by nature to English temperament and character.

Brighton, January, 1913.

Appendix

The Rules under which the following certificates are granted are added for reference.

1. Aviator Certificates.

2. Royal Aero Club Special Certificate.

3. French *Brevet Militaire*.

1
AVIATOR CERTIFICATES

The Sporting Authority governing aviation in each country represented on the F.A.I, can alone grant Aviator Certificates to candidates, of at least 18 years of age, and coming under its jurisdiction.

1. To natives, *i.e.* candidates of the same nationality as the Club.

2. To foreigners belonging to a country not represented on the F.A.I.

3. To foreigners of a country represented on the F.A.I.; but in this case the certificate can only be delivered with the authorisation of the Sporting Authority of the candidate's country.

The Royal Aero Club of the United Kingdom will grant certificates in accordance with the regulations of the *Fédération Aéronautique Internationale* to candidates who have complied with the following rules:

RULES.

1. Candidates must accomplish the three following tests:

A. Two distance flights, consisting of at least 5 kilometres (3 miles 185 yards) each in a closed circuit, the distance to be measured as described below.

B. One altitude flight, consisting of a minimum height of 50 metres (164 feet), which may form part of one of the two flight prescribed above.

2. The course on which the aviator accomplishes tests A. must be marked out by two posts situated not more than 500 metres (547 yards) apart.

3. After each turn round one of the posts the aviator must change the direction when going round the second post, so that the circuit will consist or an uninterrupted series of figures of 8.

4. The distance flown shall be reckoned as if in a straight line from post to post.

5. The method of alighting for each of the flights shall be with the motor stopped at or before the moment of touching the ground, and the aeroplane must come to rest within a distance of 50 metres (164 feet) from a point indicated previously by the candidate. The landing must be effected under normal conditions, and the officials must report the manner in which it was effected.

6. Each of the flights must be vouched for in writing by officials appointed by the Royal Aero Club. All tests to be under the control of, and in places agreed to by, the Royal Aero Club.

7. All flights must be made between sunrise and sunset, and suitable previous notice must be given to the Secretary of the Royal Aero Club.

8. The Royal Aero Club declines all responsibility for any accidents, or any damage that may occur to the aviators, their machines, or to any third parties during or in connection with the qualifying tests of the candidate.

9. Candidates must make application on a form provided for that purpose. Any expenses incurred must be borne by the candidates.

10. Foreigners belonging to a country represented on the *Fédération Aéronautique Internationale* can only receive a certificate from the Royal Aero Club after having obtained the consent of their national sporting authority, as approved by the *Fédération Aéronautique Internationale*. A certificate may be granted to

a foreigner whose country is not represented on the *Fédération Aéronautique Internationale.*

11. The Committee of the Royal Aero Club will decide if the candidate has qualified for a certificate, but reserves the right to refuse the same or withdraw the same at any time without giving reasons.

12. The decision of the Committee of the Royal Aero Club in all matters connected with the tests is final and without appeal.

13. The Committee of the Royal Aero Club may in special cases waive any or all of the above rules, and grant certificates at its discretion.

2

ROYAL AERO CLUB SPECIAL CERTIFICATE

(Under the Rules of the *Fédération Aéronautique Internationale.*)

The Royal Aero Club of the United Kingdom will grant a Special Certificate to aviators who hold the F.A.I. Aviator Certificate, who are entered on the Competitors' Register of the Royal Aero Club, and fulfil the following requirements:

(A) An altitude flight of at least 1,000 feet
rise, which shall be verified by recording barograph, sealed by the observers prior to the start.

(B) A glide from a height of at least 500 feet
above the ground to earth, with engine completely cut off. The landing must be made under normal conditions within 100 yards from the starting point. This glide may, at the candidate's option, be the conclusion of Test A. Tests A. and B. must be accomplished before Test C. is attempted.

(C) A cross-country flight, out and back round a point situated at least 50 miles from the start. The turning point will be selected by the Royal Aero Club, and will not be indicated to the candidate until one hour before the starting time selected by the candidate. This flight shall be completed within five hours of the selected starting time. No passenger may be carried during this flight.

1. A sealed barograph must be carried in all flights.

2. Each of the flights must be vouched for in writing by observ-

ers appointed by the Royal Aero Club. All tests to be under the control of, and in places agreed to by, the Royal Aero Club.

3. All flights must be made between sunrise and one hour after sunset, and suitable previous notice must be given to the Secretary of the Royal Aero Club.

4. Candidates must make application on a form provided for that purpose. Any expenses incurred must be borne by the candidates.

5. The Royal Aero Club will decide if the candidate has qualified for a certificate, but reserves the right to grant, refuse, or withdraw the same at any time without giving reasons.

6. The decision of the Royal Aero Club on all matters connected with the tests is final and without appeal.

7. The Royal Aero Club reserves itself the right to interpret, add to, amend or omit any of these rules, should it think fit.

8. The Royal Aero Club declines all responsibility for any accidents, or any damage that may occur to the aviators, their machines or to any third parties during or in connection with the qualifying tests of the candidate.

3

FRENCH *BREVET MILITAIRE*

Part 1. Practical Tests.

(a) A triangular flight of at least 200 kilometres, with the shortest side at least 20 kilometres long and with two landings at predetermined points; to be accomplished within 48 hours.

(b) A non-stop flight of 150 kilometres in a straight line to a point indicated beforehand.

(c) A similar flight but with one stop *en route*. In the course of these flights the pilot must make one flight of at least 45 minutes' duration at a minimum height of 800 metres.

Part 2. Theoretical Tests.

(a) Map reading. Meteorology, its principles. Barometrical pressure, temperature, hygrometry, clouds, and wind. Reading of meteorological charts. Utilisation of meteorological information. Air resistance, its laws.

(b) Laws of the assistance of the air applied to

aviation. Construction of aircraft. Tests on their delivery. Tuning up.

(c) Motors. Principles and working of motors.

"Brother Bosch"

Contents

To the Memory of
Captain Morritt,
Lieut. Medlicott,
Lieut. Walters,
And All Other Officers, N.C.O.'s and Men,
Who, Being Less Fortunate,
Gave Their Lives in the Endeavour.

Belovèd Country! banished from thy shore,
A stranger in this prison house of clay,
The exiled spirit weeps and sighs for thee!
Heavenward the bright perfections I adore
Direct, and the sure promise cheers the way,
That, whither love aspires, there shall my dwelling be.

Longfellow.

Note
The spelling of the word 'Bosch' was the customary one in the German prisoners' camps from which the author made his escape, and is retained for the sake of local colour.

CHAPTER 1

Captured

It was November 9th, 1916. I lay in a state of luxurious semi-consciousness pondering contentedly over things in general, transforming utter impossibilities into plausible possibilities, wondering lazily the while if I were asleep. Presently, to my disgust an indefinable, yet persistent "something" came into being, almost threatening to dispel the drowsy mist then pervading my brain. The slow thought waves gradually ceased their surging, and after a slight pause began to collect round the offending mystery, as if seeking to unravel it in a half-hearted sort of way. They gave me to understand that the "something" recurred at intervals, and even suggested that it might be a voice, though from which side of the elastic dividing line it emanated they were quite unable to say. With the consoling thought that voices often come from dreamland I allowed the whole subject to glide gently into the void and the tide of thought to continue its drugged revolutions. The next instant a noisy whirlwind swept the cobwebs away. I knew that the voice was indeed a reality, for it delivered the following message: "A very fine morning, sir!"

Obviously my dutiful servant desired me to rise and enjoy the full benefit of the beautiful day. Agreeing with Harry Lauder, that "*It's nice to get up in the morning, but it's nicer to stay in bed!*" I am sorry to say I cunningly dismissed the orderly with a few false assurances, turned over on my side and promptly forgot all about such trivial matters. Conscience was kicking very feebly, and just as sleep was about to return, the air commenced to vibrate and something swept overhead with a whirling roar—an "early bird" testing the air. Galvanised into action by this knowledge, I sprang out of bed, and seizing whatever garments happened to be the nearest, was half dressed before I had even time to yawn!

Then snatching up my map, coat, hat, and goggles, I burst from the hut and began slithering along the duck-boards towards the hangars, at the same time endeavouring to fasten the unwilling hooks of my Flying Corps tunic and devoutly hoping that I should not be late for the bomb raid. For weeks we had been standing by for this raid in particular, the object of which was to bomb Douai aerodrome. This was a particularly warm spot to fly over, for in these days it was regarded as the home of "Archies" and the latest hostile aircraft. It is, therefore, not surprising that the general feeling of the squadron was that the sooner it was over the better for all concerned. Arrived at the sheds I was relieved to find that I was in good time, at all events. The machines (two-seater artillery machines, then commonly known as "Quirks") were lined up on the aerodrome with bomb racks loaded, their noses to the wind, awaiting the signal to ascend. I saluted the C.O., waved to a friend or two and climbed into the pilot's seat of my waiting machine. Then, adjusting the levers, I signified to the waiting mechanics that I was ready for them to "suck in" (an operation necessary prior to the starting of the engine).

Having made sure that everything was O.K. and waited for the others to ascend, I took off and, after climbing steadily for some time, took up my specified position in the formation. For some time we circled about over a pre-arranged rendezvous, until joined by an escort of fighting machines and another squadron of bombers, and then settled down to business. Flying straight into the sun we soon arrived at and passed over the irregular spidery lines of trenches (those on Vimy Ridge showing up particularly clearly), and continued forging ahead, past many familiar landmarks, always in the direction of Douai. I for one never dreamt of being taken prisoner and had every intention of making a record breakfast on my return. My engine was going rather badly, but the odds were that it would see me through.

Only too soon the anti-aircraft started their harassing fire, throwing up a startling number of nerve-racking, high explosive shells, each one a curling black sausage of hate and steel splinters. When we were some way over my machine lagged behind the rest. The engine spluttered intermittently and could not be induced to go at all well. As my machine became more isolated I cast anxious glances about and was soon rewarded by seeing two wicked little enemy scouts waiting for an easy prey (at that time they did not usually attack a formation, but waited behind for the likes o' me). While one scout attracted my attention on the left and I was engaged in keeping him off by firing occasional bursts, a machine gun opened fire with a deafening clatter at point-blank range from behind.

In an instant the surrounding air became full of innumerable tiny, brilliant flames, passing me at an incredible speed like minute streaks of lightning, each one giving forth a curious *staccato* whistling crack as it plunged through or beside the tormented machine, leaving in its wake a thin curling line of blue smoke. I was in the middle of a relentless storm of burning tracer bullets, vying one with the other for the honour of passing through the petrol tank, thereby converting my machine into a seething furnace. Having no observer to defend my tail I turned steeply to meet my new adversary.

However, before completing the manoeuvre I received another deadly burst of fire, which, though it somehow missed me, shot away several of my control wires. What happened next I cannot be sure, but the machine seemed to turn over, and my machine gun fell off with a crash. This took place at an altitude of six thousand feet. My next impression was that I seemed to be in the centre of a whirling vortex, around which all creation revolved at an extraordinary speed, and realised that my trusty steed was indulging in a particularly violent "spinning nose dive." A "spin" at the best of times rather takes one's breath away, so, shutting the throttle, I endeavoured to come out of it in the usual way. To my surprise, the engine refused to slow down, or any of the controls to respond, except one, which only tended to make matters worse.

The one thing left to be done was to "switch off" and trust to luck. This, however, was more easily decided on than accomplished, for by this time the machine was plunging to earth so rapidly, with the engine full on, that I felt as if I were tied to a peg-top, which was being hurled downwards with irresistible force. Fighting blindly against the tremendous air-pressure, which rendered me hardly able to move, I forced my left arm, inch by inch, along the edge of the "cockpit" until I succeeded in turning the switch lever downwards. A glance at the speedometer did not reassure me, the poor thing seemed very much overworked. Descending very rapidly I kept getting a glimpse of a pretty red-roofed village, which became ominously more distinct at every plunging revolution.

I vaguely thought there would be rather a splash when we arrived at our destination, but at eight hundred feet Providence came to the rescue. I heard the welcome cessation of the wild screaming hum of the strained wires. After switching on, the engine informed me with much spluttering that it was sorry that I should have to land on the wrong side, but it really had done its best. I had just managed to turn towards our trenches, when the scout pilot, seeing I did not land, at once followed me down and with its machine gun impressed on me that the sooner I landed the better. As I was then a long way over the lines, sinking fast towards the tree-tops, I had no alternative, so endeavoured to reach the village green. By this time the machine was literally riddled with bullets, though, luckily, I had not been touched. Before landing I overtook a German horseman, so thinking to introduce myself I dived on him from a low altitude, just passing over his head.

Well, scare him I certainly did, poor man; he was much too frightened to get off, and seemed to be doing his best to get inside his would-be Trojan animal. The machine landed on a heap of picks and shovels, ran among a number of Huns who were having a morning wash at some troughs (or rather I should say, a lick and a promise!). They scattered and then closed in on the machine. I ran one wing into a post, and tried the lighter, which did not work. I was a prisoner. Undoubtedly, the next German *communiqué* announced that the gallant Lieutenant X. had brought down his thirtieth machine; it is probable that this gallant officer had heard strange rumours of what lay behind the British lines, but preferred cruising on the safer side. I could hardly believe that these grey-clad, rather unshaven men who jabbered excitedly were genuine "Huns." I was furious and very "fed-up," but that did not help, so turning in my seat and raising my hand I said, "*Gutten Morgen.*" This surprised them so much that they forgot to be rude and mostly returned the compliment.

Chapter 2

Cambrai

The immediate treatment I received was rather better than I had expected. Several officers came forward, and one, who held a revolver, told me in broken English to get out. So leaving my poor old machine, we proceeded to the village headquarters.

Photographers appeared from nowhere and I was twice "snapped" on the way, though I'm afraid I did not act up to the usual request, "look pleasant." On arriving at a small house I was received by a German general, who looked rather like an Xmas tree, the Iron Crosses were so numerous. As I stood to attention he politely inquired if I spoke German, even condescending to smile faintly when I replied, "*Ja, un peu!*" At first when I answered a few preliminary questions he was politeness itself. He then asked for my squadron number, to which I could only reply that I was sorry but could not answer him, whereupon he pointed out that it was of no military value whatever, and that it was only to assist in my identification in the report of my capture which would go to England. So thoughtful of him; such a plausible excuse!

Of course I remained silent, whereupon "*la politesse*" vanished and an angry Hun took its place. He screamed, threatened, and waved his arms about, but as I did not seem very impressed at the display, he rushed out of the room, slamming the door and not returning. Oh, for a "movie" camera! A Flying Corps officer then took me in a car to an aerodrome, and told me I should have lunch with the officers at the *château*, where they were quartered. Here I met about nine German airmen, who greeted me in a typically foreign manner. They seemed quite a nice lot on the whole, though I did not know them long enough to really form an opinion. Soon a good German gramophone was playing and lunch began. The food was rather poor, but champagne plentiful.

During the meal the gramophone, which was nearest to me, finished a record, so getting up I changed the needle and started the other side. But it wasn't the "Bing Boys" this time! Strange to say, they were quite astonished at this performance, thinking, perhaps, that I could not change the needle. Afterwards, at coffee, a lieutenant asked me what we thought of their flying corps, to which I replied that I thought it was all right. He seemed quite prepared for this, and hastily said that I must remember that they had fewer machines. I think it must have occurred to every captured airman how splendid it would be to steal an enemy aeroplane and fly back, then after a graceful landing report to the C.O. that you had returned. These flights are not infrequently pleasurably accomplished in imagination, but such opportunities do not often, if ever, present themselves.

Just before leaving the *château*, I excused myself and got as far as the back door, where I had to explain to some German orderlies that I was only trying to find my coat. I was taken by car to corps headquarters at another *château*, where I saw some young officers, elegantly dressed, lounging about. After much useless bowing and scraping I was again interrogated by an objectionable colonel, but they seemed used to failure, and soon ceased their efforts. A major who assisted spoke English well, and made himself quite pleasant till I left. On hearing that I was in the Devons he told me that on leaving the university his father had sent him to live at a small village near Barnstaple, where he had remained for several years.

Doubtless, a hard-working man of leisure! He seemed a very able officer, but decidedly young for a German major. On being told that all leather goods were confiscated, I was forced to give up my Sam Brown belt much against my will. They seemed very familiar with the movements of our troops, and I noticed that though their telephones were rather large and clumsy they carried slight sounds very distinctly, so much so, that when at the other end of the room I could hear practically the whole conversation.

Towards evening the major told me to get ready to go to Cambrai, and at the same time said, that as my leather flying coat was also confiscated they had cut off the fur collar, which he then handed back. This rather annoyed me, so I told him to keep it, which incident I regretted afterwards. However, he lent me a German coat, which was some comfort. On the way to Cambrai we again passed near the lines, some British star shells being plainly visible. What a difference a few kilometres make! The Germans depend on their railway transport more than we do. Certainly their road transport cannot be compared with ours. We passed a few cars and motor lorries, the majority giving one the impression that they were falling to bits, so noisy and shabby were they. I only saw two or three motor cyclists the whole time, and those I did see rode machines of an antiquated pattern. We passed a lot of horse transport, nearly all the ambulances in the district being horse drawn. Most cars, including our own, were only capable of emitting useless squeaks on emergencies.

Soon we entered Cambrai, an old, picturesque French town, and drew up at the entrance to the citadel, where a guard allowed us to enter. I was then left with a Lieutenant Schram, the intelligence officer, who gave me coffee and cigars and plied me with questions. He was very anxious to discover all he could about our tanks, and possessed many supposed models, mostly not in the least like them. He emphasised the opinion that, of course we should not get Bapaume, at the same time allowing he thought there might be a moving battle in the spring. From his conversation I gathered that they were very familiar with formation and movements of most of our Colonial units.

The *tête-à-tête* at an end, I was taken to my quarters, a bare whitewashed room, containing one French flying officer, two British lieutenants, if I remember rightly, both in the D.L.I., having been taken near Bapaume, and also a Canadian sergeant-major. It is unnecessary to say how pleased I was to see them. Someone had acquired a portion of an old magazine, which was much sought after, it being the only means of passing the time. Our sleeping accommodation consisted of two old straw mattresses, one on the floor and the other on a shelf above.

Being tired we slept soundly, but in the morning we were horrified to find we had not been alone, but that quite a varied menagerie had shared our couches with us. Why the blankets did not run away in the night I cannot think. The Huns promised to have lots of things done but never did anything, in fact, they lie as easily as they breathe, even when there is nothing to be gained by it.

A comparatively nice N.C.O. was in charge of us, called Nelson! We afterwards learnt that his father had been English, and that his own knowledge of England appeared to be confined to an Oxford restaurant. One day when our lunch, consisting of black and watery soup, was brought up he sympathetically remarked that it was a pity we could not have chicken and ham. I wonder what he would have done had someone enticingly rattled a shilling on a plate?

During the day we were allowed to walk round the barrack square for about three hours with eighty British and a hundred and fifty French soldiers, some of whom were daily detailed to work in the town. I noticed that the Germans were inclined to treat our soldiers the worst, frequently shouting threats at them in their guttural language. In the evenings I sometimes managed to get downstairs with the men, and in this way was able to join in some impromptu singsongs. Sanitary arrangements were very bad and disinfectants unknown. We were allowed to buy a little extra bread and some turnip jam at exorbitant prices, which helped us considerably, as breakfast consisted only of luke-warm acorn coffee, lunch of a weird soup containing *sauerkraut* or barley, supper of soup or tea alternate days. We amused ourselves by carving our names on the table, or by drawing regimental crests or pictures of Hun aeroplanes descending in flames, in out of the way corners.

On being told that toothbrushes were out of stock (I do not think they ever were in), I manufactured a homemade one on boy scout lines. It consisted of a small bundle of twigs and splinters tied together (like a young besom), and though it did its work well, the morning sweep was decidedly painful.

CHAPTER 3

Adventure No. 1

After remaining there a week we were told that we should leave the next morning for Germany, which we should grow to like very much! During our stay, except for a few exciting intervals when British machines passed over the town, we had plenty of time for meditation, and usually when darkness fell could see by the gun flashes that the evening strafe was in progress. This always reminded me of an argument which had once taken place in our squadron mess, late one evening before turning in, during which I had expressed the opinion that should anyone with infantry experience be forced to land the wrong side just before dark, provided he could avoid Huns, it might be just possible for him to return the next night through the trenches. Now I felt it was up to me to prove it should such an opportunity present itself.

Cambrai citadel is both solid and imposing, and must have proved itself a formidable fortress. Crowning a slight eminence, it overlooks most of the town. On the three sides are ramparts, varying from about twenty to sixty feet in height, while on a fourth it is now bounded by barbed wire and high railings, with only a slight drop on the other side. At the main entrance the road crosses the old moat and passes under a massive archway which adjoins the guardroom. All the approaches to the outer walls are guarded by quantities of barbed wire and numerous sentries.

After a thorough search I at last discovered a small round hole in the wall of an outbuilding near the roof, through which I decided it would be possible to squeeze, in the dusk, unobserved by the sentry. The new German coat I had received on the way had been again in its turn exchanged for an old French one. This I took to the men's quarters and, finally, after hunting the whole place, found an old German coat hanging up. After bargaining for some time I made my fourth exchange, and returned successful. Later in the afternoon an English N.C.O. told me that he had heard of my search and presented me with an old German fatigue cap which had been unearthed somewhere by his pals.

Now having everything ready I determined to try my luck about six o'clock that evening before being shut up for the night. After learning some new German words likely to be of use, such as "wire entanglements," "dugouts," etc., I returned to my room and waited. My plan was to follow the gun flashes, which in all probability would lead me to the Bapaume area, where I expected to find some wire or wooden posts, which I should carry with me as I approached the lines, and endeavour to avoid suspicion by mingling with working parties as an engineer. If thus far successful I hoped to repair the German wire entanglements, which in this district were much damaged by our shell fire, and eventually slip away and get into touch with our patrols.

At a quarter to six a German flying officer entered our room and invited me to dinner at their Cambrai headquarters, assuring me that there would be plenty to eat and drink. (I expect after skilfully mixed drinks they hoped to loosen my tongue. When a Hun lays himself out to be pleasant it is almost certain that in some way he expects to benefit by it.) If you wish to realise how tempting this offer was, live on a watery starvation diet for eight days and then be given the opportunity of a good meal. However, when I excused myself on the plea of being a little unwell, "*Mein freund*" was quite non-plussed. While he was still trying to extract information, unsuccessfully, from the others, I left the room after pocketing a slice of bread.

Once in the outhouse I chose my time and, climbing up to the hole in the wall, squeezed myself through with difficulty, for it was only just large enough. When the sentry's back was turned I dropped to the ground on the other side, about ten feet below, making considerable noise. I was now past the line of barbed wire, but there still remained the ramparts to negotiate. Never having been able to see over this point from our quarters we had no means of ascertaining the drop to the ground below. The corner of the ramparts I was making for was under forty yards away, but it took me about three-quarters of an hour to get there, crawling on crackling dry leaves under the shadow of the wall. The slightest noise would probably have attracted the sentry's attention and caused him to switch on the electric light, which they all carry slung round their necks.

Oh! what a noise those leaves made! Just before I got to the wall I heard rather a commotion outside the guardroom, and although expecting to get at least a night's start before my absence was discovered, concluded that I had already been missed. (Afterwards I found that this was indeed the case, as the German flying officer on leaving had told the *commandant* that I was unwell; a doctor was then sent up, but I could not be found.) Getting up, I ran to the wall and looked over. In the dusk I faintly distinguished some bushes below. The glance was not reassuring, but "the die was cast," and over I went. I shall always remember that horrible sensation of falling. It took longer than I expected to reach the ground. Instantaneously there flashed through my brain a formula I had learnt at school, *i.e.*, that an object falling increases its velocity thirty-two feet per second. I now realised for the first time how true it was.

The drop was somewhere between twenty and thirty feet. Just near the ground my fall was broken by my being suspended for the fraction of a second on some field telephone wires, which broke and deposited me in the centre of a laurel bush, which split in half with a crash. It is not so much the fall but the sudden stop which does the damage. My breath being knocked out of me and seeing several floating stars of great brilliance, I vaguely wondered if I were dead, but I was considerably relieved to find that this was not the case. No bones broken, only some bruises. As I was getting to my feet I heard some one coming down a gravel path which passed beside me. Crouching down, I saw it was a civilian, who proceeded to light a cigar and passed on. I followed suit by lighting my one and only cigarette, and after cutting a stick, entered a darkened street, externally a perfectly good Hun.

But even German soldiers are subject to restrictions and I might be asked questions. Consequently, my one idea was to get out of the town as quickly as possible. I met two French women, to whom I explained my position, and asked the nearest way into the country. They were frightened and unwilling to talk at first, but when I opened my coat and showed them the British uniform underneath, they pointed to a road which I followed. Soon the town was left behind and I was making for the gun-flashes and crossing a turnip field. Swinging along at a good pace the turnip-tops whipped my boots and made quite a noise. Suddenly a challenge rang out from a small railway bridge. "*Halt! Wer da!*" (On these occasions it seems as if one's heart has been put to the wrong use, it being really fashioned to be a pendulum for a grandfather clock.)

The next second an electric light was switched on, but I had already fallen among the turnips, endeavouring to make a noise like one (a turnip). Then ensued an interesting silence fraught with many possibilities. Did the turnip's voice deceive the Hun? At any rate the light was soon turned off, much to my relief; then quietly I slipped away. After about an hour's walking across country I came to what I supposed to be a stream, showing up in the moonlight, with a few bushes growing along the side. Walking parallel to it for a few yards and not seeing a bridge, I thought it might be quite shallow, so tested it with a stick. Imagine my pleasant surprise when I found that it was not water at all, but a narrow white concrete path, evidently newly made. I noticed that nearly all roads running parallel to the front had a very deep trench dug on the east (German) side. Presumably, these were later used considerably when we were engaged in shelling the roads.

Soon I came to the Cambrai Canal, which had to be crossed, and as it was the middle of November it gave me the shivers even to look at the dark water. After walking some distance down the tow-path, I encountered a Hun. Though not feeling at all bold I said, "*G'nacht*," which I felt sounded feeble, though I knew it to be the correct thing in some parts of Germany. To this he replied, "*Abend*" (evening). (Quite a valuable lesson in the usual custom among soldiers.)

Skirting a few houses and a timber yard I approached a large well-built iron railway bridge spanning the canal. Climbing over some barbed wire I cautiously mounted the embankment. Looking along the bridge I saw there were two lines separated by some arched iron girders. From recent experience I knew that this must be strongly guarded, but reasoned that if I closely followed a train I should in all probability find the line free for a few seconds. Presently a freight train came rumbling along, and I rushed after it in a whirl of air, in my haste almost being knocked down by the end carriages. As the bridge was rather long and the train going fast, in a very short time I was being left stranded.

When I was nearing the other side I stopped an instant to listen. It was just as well I did. Not more than three yards away, on the other side of the ironwork, a man spoke in German and was immediately answered by another, who turned on his light and commenced walking towards the end of the bridge I was making for, to return to his old beat on my line. There was no time to lose, so rushing back on tiptoe and down the embankment I fell over the barbed wire at the bottom, which painfully impressed on me its disapproval of my conduct.

After following the canal for a few hundred yards there seemed no alternative but to swim across, so in I went, greatcoat and all. It was awfully cold. At first my clothes and fleeced-lined flying boots held the air and supported me, so that I lay on the surface of the water as if bathing in the Dead Sea, feeling very ridiculous. But only too soon everything filled up and I felt like a stone. Swimming as silently as possible, I had almost reached the opposite bank, feeling very tired, when I saw something glisten just in front which looked very like a bayonet, and a man's voice shouted "*Hier*." Picture the situation: a dark but starry November night, Hun sentry guarding barges, and a poor wretch floundering about in the water, then you will not be surprised that my heart after jumping into my mouth, worked overtime again! The Hun thought I was a dog; I must be one without delay if I wished to preserve a whole skin, so after a spluttering growl I turned back with new energy, swimming like a dog and whining softly.

After again calling to me several times he threw a few things in my direction, which fortunately went wide. I then swam round a barge and with a great effort pulled myself out of the water, rewarding the Hun, who was now calling a friend, with a final bark. I ran across a field with the water pouring from me. I did not think one could be so cold, an icicle was warm in comparison! With numb fingers I wrung some of the water out of my clothes, and with chattering teeth considered the situation. Here I was, still on the wrong side—the only thing left to try was a village bridge. Again following the tow-path I neared some lights, which proved to be a hospital, and found myself in an apparently unoccupied station-yard, among a number of large heaps. On raising a corner of a tarpaulin which covered the nearest I recognised the familiar wicker crates, which contained something heavy. It was an ammunition dump! I soon found the name of the station on the deserted platform—Mannièrs.

As I was leaving the dump, thinking of a possible future, and what a lovely explosion one well-directed bomb would make, I heard someone coming towards me. At once hopping off the road I crouched against one of the shell heaps where the darkness was more dense, my weight causing the wicker to creak. But the seemingly deaf individual passed by and I breathed again. Entering the main village street at a good pace, whistling a German tune, I was accosted by two Huns carrying a heavy basket on a stick. One inquired of me the way to some headquarters. I dared not stop, so turning my head, growled out a sullen "*Ich weiss nicht*" (I don't know). They seemed grieved at my bad manners, but were soon left behind.

Although it was very late a number of troops were still singing uproariously in the various *estaminets* which I passed. On turning a corner I saw the village bridge and on it a sentry box. While I stood in the dark shadow of a house a small party of Germans, carrying saddlery, overtook me. Tacking myself on casually behind some of them we all passed over the bridge quite happily, and feeling in a cheeky mood I wished the sentry "good evening."

Once more I was passing swiftly over the country, devoutly hoping there would not be any more canals. Several hours passed uneventfully. Some of the concrete paths leading in the right direction afforded excellent walking. They were mostly new and appeared to be only laid on the mud without any foundation. On a small rise I came upon a trench system under construction (probably the now famous Hindenburg line), which I examined. The few dug-outs I saw were incomplete, the trenches rather wet and shallow and not yet sandbagged.

After crossing two lines of more or less continuous trenches I inspected the wire entanglements, wooden posts (charred, so as not to show up in aerial photographs) and iron corkscrews which were already in position, but only a little fine and barbed wire as yet, which was quite easy to get through. Although the firing had died down it continued sufficiently to enable me to keep my direction. Just as I was leaving these trenches behind my progress was arrested by a sudden jerk, and I found myself lying face downwards full length in the mud. A carefully laid wire had tripped its first "*Engländer!*" I was now plastered with mud from head to foot, and getting up in a very bad temper determined that at least that portion of wire should not interfere with another Britisher. After a short struggle I succeeded in tearing it up and went on my way somewhat appeased.

The front was now quite quiet, and after many falls, footsore and tired, I came to a large wood (the Bois de Logeost) a little before dawn. In this I hoped to find cover for the day, but it was full of transport, and many dim lights proclaimed the presence of huts. I had been walking parallel to it for some distance when a British aeroplane dropped some bombs too close to be pleasant, causing quite a stir in the wood, shortly followed by an anti-aircraft gun opening fire not far away. I have never felt so small in my life, and while tramping on in a dejected manner, in imagination I was flying once again over the lines, the occupied territory lying below me like a map: but in spite of the tranquillity of the scene (for in this pleasant dream not a gun was in action) I became conscious of a disturbing element somewhere, something was out of place. To what was it due?

Then all at once I realised that it was all connected with an infinitesimal object which wandered aimlessly about among the German batteries, and yet attracted every one's attention. Vaguely I wondered what it could be? Then the dream slowly faded, and as reality took its place I knew that I was that atom! When things were quiet again I distinctly heard plonk, plonk, plonk, the sound made by hand grenades, rising from the lower ground in front, this was soon followed by the fainter cracking of a machine gun and a brilliant Verey light, which I concluded was from three to four miles away. All at once, just beside me, there was a blinding flash, immediately followed by a deafening roar and the screaming hiss of a shell, the latter lasting several seconds, then slowly dying away into the night with a sigh. One of the German heavies had fired from a neighbouring clump of trees. Had my skin been any looser I should certainly have jumped out of it. Very soon I heard the distant explosion of the bursting shell—*Cr—ump*, and then dashed off in the opposite direction.

Chapter 4

Retaken

The country was very bare and the lines so close that there were no hay or straw stacks about. The stars were beginning to fade from the sky, so hastily retracing my steps for about a mile, in search of cover, I almost fell over a tiny straw heap in the middle of a field. It was close to a village, but as no tracks passed anywhere near it I decided that this should be my hiding place for the day. After eating the remains of the black bread, now a sloppy mass in my pocket, I emptied the water which still remained in my flying-boots and placed them in a side of the heap to dry, just below the surface. Wrapping my slightly drier overcoat round my feet for warmth, I wormed my way into the centre, and pulled the straw after me.

The bottom of the heap was wet and contained mice, which squeaked when my teeth stopped chattering for a few seconds. I tried meowing, but they were not taken in for long! Sleep was out of the question, and there was nothing else to do but watch the cold grey fingers of light creeping through the wet straw. From my knowledge of the front, I gathered that I had arrived north of my objective, where the Huns were expecting our next attack, and the trenches were strongly held. Had I a sporting chance or were the odds against me too great? If the latter was the case and it was impossible, I prayed that I might be recaptured before making the attempt the next night.

The minutes passed like hours, but at last the sun rose, evidently very much against its will. About ten o'clock next morning I faintly heard the thud of horse's hoofs approaching at a canter from the direction of the village. At first I thought nothing of it, but as these grew rapidly louder and louder, my uneasiness increased and I lay perfectly still under the straw. The horse came straight to my heap, and stopped dead at the German word of command, "*R-r-r-r*" (whoa!). Soon the rider uttered an exclamation and, leaning over, drew out a flying boot, to my dismay, but as this was wet, muddy and old looking he soon threw it down again.

In the meantime the horse kept sniffing and nibbling at the straw which thinly covered my face, and I felt inclined to repeat to myself an old nursery rhyme: "*Fe, fi, fo, fum, I smell the blood of an Englishman!*" As the brute continued blowing the straw from my face, I tried to make him desist by returning the compliment by blowing back at him. He jumped and threw up his head, but now his curiosity being thoroughly aroused returned to his explorations with renewed vigour, partly uncovering me. I did not move, but knew that the game was up when the rider drew his breath in sharply. Looking up I saw surprise written on every feature of the bearded Hun N.C.O. He was a thick-set man with a revolver holster at his belt. I had no chance of resistance, as the country was quite open and my boots were off, so sitting up I greeted him with a "*Gutten Morgen.*" He saw that I was an English "*Flieger*" (airman), but firmly refused to believe that I was an officer. He told me I was near Achiet-le-Petit, and then motioned me to go with him to the village, which I did. (An account of the foregoing episode appeared in the German papers later.)

We went straight to the village headquarters, where there were several officers spotlessly dressed in blue or field-grey, against which my tramp-like appearance formed a strange contrast. They were quite decent, with one exception, a sour-looking captain, and were rather amused than otherwise, even allowing a Frenchwoman to make me some coffee. When I remarked on the wonderful way in which the Germans had traced me from Cambrai, they laughed and said my discovery was purely accidental, the N.C.O. having been detailed to find some straw for the transport.

I was sent back to Cambrai in a wagon with an armed guard of three, exclusive of the driver and the mounted N.C.O. I was very annoyed on being told that the latter would receive the Iron Cross, and tried to impress on them that my discovery was entirely due to the horse, who deserved a bran mash. It was bitterly cold and, on passing through every village, I was made to remove my coat to show the inhabitants that I was a prisoner. I was quite pleased when we arrived at our destination.

The commandant received me with a growl, and I was taken to the guardroom, where the same Hun N.C.O. casually informed me that I was to be shot. In an unconvincing way I told myself this was nonsense. The next move was not at all reassuring. I was marched through the back door into a tiny courtyard, accompanied by the sergeant of the guard and several privates armed with rifles! I am glad to say that the bluff was soon over, and I was put into a half dark stone cell. In a short time I was fished out to see Lieutenant Schram, who told me that I was the first to escape from there, but that I should never get another opportunity. He went on to say that when my disappearance had been discovered the previous evening, it was thought that I had closely followed the flying officer who had asked me to dinner when he left through the main gate, until the broken wires were found. Men and trained dogs had then endeavoured to trace me, but that, unfortunately, they had all gone the wrong way!

When I was taken back at the end of the interview, a sergeant-major and a corporal thought they would have some fun at my expense. They opened my cell door and then led me to a comparatively comfortable room close by, and asked me which I preferred. However, I upset their calculations by entering my original cell and sitting down. As the result of an argument which ensued I was put into the better room, where I fell asleep. This comfort was only short-lived, and soon, by order of the commandant, I was put into the original cell again.

It snowed all the next evening, and when the sergeant brought me my watery supper, I asked if he would stand my boots by the guard-room fire that night as the fleece held such a quantity of water. He seemed surprised at my request, but said that he would ask. He soon returned and said that it could not be done. It was four days before I felt at all warm, my clothes drying on me all the time. I have since been told that Lieutenant Schram, while speaking of me later to other captured officers, asserted that he dried all my clothes for me. Yet this same gentleman during his first interrogation asked me why we English called them uncultured!

On the afternoon of the fourth day I was ordered to get ready to proceed to Germany, as enough prisoners had been captured at the Beaumont Hamel show to make up a large draft. At the main entrance I found a group of about twenty officers, composed of eight or ten *Zouaves* and the remainder British. Then off we went to the station in high spirits, for it is not often that one gets a chance of a tour in Germany, *via* France and Belgium, free of charge!

CHAPTER 5

Osnabrück

Our guards had mostly been selected from different regiments, on account of their being due for leave in Germany. The officer in charge travelled separately. He had recently been wounded, and had seen rather more of the British than he cared; in consequence he was almost human! Not yet being dry and now having no overcoat, I felt decidedly cold. We arrived late at St. Quentin and settled down for a long wait, but our good spirits were infectious and, besides, some of our number had with them a surplus of turnip jam, and we were allowed to sing. This we did with a vengeance, and it was indeed curious to hear the desolate waiting-room echoing the popular strains of: "Pack up your troubles in your old kit bag, and smile, smile, smile."

This *impromptu* concert delighted the French, who joined in as best they could. Soon we had quite a little audience of solitary Huns, who peeped through the open door and listened to the "Mad English," open-mouthed. At last the express steamed in from the south-east and in quite an exhausted condition we were graciously shown in to second-class compartments in a way which clearly said "Second class is much too good for you."

After a tedious journey, during which we received something to eat, we arrived at Cologne about eleven o'clock the next morning. The station contained almost every variety of Hun. These people represented the cowards who in 1914 had flung stones at and otherwise insulted those brave men of our old regular army, who stopped at this station, packed in cattle trucks like animals, mostly wounded and dying. Nearly two years of war have passed since then, bringing with them suffering and a certain refining influence which had not altogether been without its effect. Now, though most of them stared rudely, few showed signs of open hostility. Following our officer down some steps and winding subways, we were approaching a large restaurant, when a rather senior Hun officer ran after us, cursing us in German for not saluting him when we had passed him on the platform! One of the British replied, "*Nix verstand*" (*No compris*). Whereupon he went away thoroughly disgusted.

One of our party, a major of the 9th Zouaves, who spoke German very well, asked if we might have some refreshments, to which the officer acquiesced. We entered a large and almost unoccupied room separated from the main dining-hall by a glass screen, and took up our positions at a table by the window. Immediately outside towered the famous cathedral, shutting out most of the sky, the spires and countless pinnacles showing up to great advantage in the sunshine. Soon a waiter appeared with a menu containing a list of weird dishes, the most popular of which was a very thin slice of sausage reposing on a very large slice of black bread. This cost one *mark* (but perhaps they saw us coming!). Great excitement was caused when someone found it was possible to obtain goose, but as our very limited supply of money was almost exhausted this had to be ruled out.

The fish salad when it arrived was *peculiarly* nasty. It was almost raw and had an overpowering flavour of mud! Beer did not seem to be allowed, but a tip soon settled that, and we all received large glasses of light lager. The people in the hall were a funny-looking crowd but quite amusing to watch, mostly drinking quantities of beer and regarding us with sullen curiosity through the glass screen. The majority of the men were ugly and square-headed, with closely-cropped hair, reminding one of a group of convicts. Some of the girls, however, gave us encouraging smiles.

When the bills were being settled up, there strode in an angry German major, complete with helmet and sword, who entered into a violent conversation with our unfortunate officer, who stood at the salute most of the time. After making a noise like a dog fight he departed with a final gesticulation in our direction. We did not know what the row was about, but suppose that the officer in charge had been thus strafed in public, either for bringing us there or allowing us to have beer. At any rate, we were hurried out to await our train on the platform. A small circle soon formed round us, largely made up of sailors, whom we concluded must be on indefinite leave.

As our train was steaming up a civilian gave vent to his feelings by fixing his evil eyes upon us and at the same time moving his lips with a deadly purpose, cursing us inaudibly. I should never have thought a face could express such condensed hatred. He must have been conversing with his Satanic Master. However, as we only smiled sweetly in return, he cannot have felt much satisfaction. Before getting into our train we spent our last few *pfennigs* buying sweets at an automatic slot machine. The acquired sweets were wrapped in a paper covering, on which different notices were printed, the majority were to this effect:

Remember the shameful *Baralong* outrage, in punishment for which our airships shall devastate the Eastern Counties of England and destroy London.

We showed this to our guards, who firmly believed that it would shortly come to pass, and could not understand our amusement. A few minutes out from Cologne, as we went rushing over a long iron bridge, we celebrated our crossing the Rhine by winding up our watches and singing the popular song: "When we've wound up the watch on the Rhine."

In the late afternoon the train passed through Essen, the blast furnaces casting a lurid light on the surrounding country. Travelling northwards we ran into snow, which, when we alighted was quite deep. This was our destination, Osnabrück. At first it looked as if we should have to walk to the camp, but the German officer was, luckily, able to hire two brakes, and away we went. Osnabrück is an old town with a population of about 60,000. We drove past numbers of children and dogs revelling in the first winter sports, utterly regardless of their country's serious condition. On our arrival an officer and several N.C.O.'s took all particulars and descriptions. It was only then that I discovered, to my astonishment, that my eyes were blue.

Next we found a hot shower-bath in store for us, during which procedure all our clothes were taken away on the excuse that they were to be disinfected. We enjoyed the bath very much and were longing for a clean change, but were disgusted to find that this was not forthcoming, and that we had to put on the same torn and muddy clothes once more, which the Huns had only removed to search. We were then locked in a room for ten days and told that we were in quarantine, no account being taken of the three weeks or a month that some of us had already spent in the German lines. The whole thing was a farce. We could then buy a change of underclothing, and daily consumed prodigious quantities of Dutch chocolate, also procurable from the canteen (which I afterwards bought in Holland for one-tenth of the price).

Some of the British who had been in the camp for some time managed to get books and a little food in to us. A great deal of our time was occupied in making out orders for things we wanted from home, edibles taking by far the most important part. Every evening after supper we always drank the King's health in tea. Though the quality of the beverage was weak, our loyalty had never been stronger. When extra dull our home-made band played some rousing selection; my special instrument required much skill, and consisted of the dust-bin lid and a poker. The climax was reached one day when the sentry entered with a paper from the canteen, announcing that the British claimed to have shot down two Zeppelins in flames over London.

Eventually the tenth day passed and we were free to go in with the others, who at once made us welcome. Owing to the monotony of camp life it is very difficult to write a consecutive account of the daily routine, which would be of any interest to the reader. I shall therefore only outline certain points under various headings, which I venture to hope may not prove a source of boredom, judging from the numerous questions contained in letters of enquiry directed to me.

Accommodation.—The main three-storey building was a convert-ed German artillery barracks, with the gravelled courtyards used for exercising divided by a disused riding-school. The prisoners consisted of about seventy-five French, living on the ground floor, and eighty-five British, mostly R.F.C., taken at the Somme, living on the second floor, and from one hundred and fifty to two hundred Russians on the third. The rooms each contained from four to ten beds, according to the size, which we usually stacked two deep so that they should take up as little space as possible. With the aid of wall paper, deck chairs, ta-blecloths and the like, obtainable at the canteen, together with pictures from home, some of the rooms looked very cosy indeed.

Each one contained a stove, which at first we were able to keep well supplied, as it was possible to buy coal in addition to the ration, though latterly there was a considerable shortage. Mattresses were either spring or made of old straw, and sometimes contained little creepy-crawlies. My record evening catch numbered twenty-five, and this little collection afforded some exciting races. By the way, I might add that if one puts a match to them they go off "*pop*." The Germans rendered slight assistance, but the Keating's contained in our parcels soon got them under way. The sanitary conditions were not good, but I must admit to having seen a little disinfectant.

Part of the time we were allowed a common room of our own, but latterly had to share one with the Russians. Washing was sent to the town weekly. A medical orderly was on the premises during the day, and a doctor came two or three times a week. Before leaving we were inoculated against smallpox, typhoid and cholera. This was a most obnoxious proceeding which took place every six or seven days, until the doctor had jabbed us all six times in the chest with his confounded needle. French and Russian orderlies were provided, each detailed to look after one or two rooms.

Recreation.—At first it was possible to play football, but that was soon stopped. Rackets, boxing and a sort of cricket were played in the riding-school; once or twice a week we organised a concert or a dance, theatrical costumes being hired from the town on parole. The Russians had a really first-class *mandoline* and *balalaika* band, with which they played many of their waltzes and curiously attractive folk-songs. During these concerts a certain Englishman solemnly sang some new Russian songs, learnt by heart, of which he did not understand a word. A young Russian used to make up into a delightful girl, who, with a partner, danced a cake-walk, accompanied by the blare of their new brass band. *Mandolines* were soon in vogue and most rooms could boast of several. As we were mostly beginners the resulting noise is best left to the imagination. Whist drives, bridge tournaments, etc., helped to pass the time, and a good many of us improved the shining hour by learning French, Russian or German in exchange for lessons in our own language.

The winter brought with it many snow fights, and a successful slide which I started, though popular, resulted in many bumps and bruises. The bottom of the slide led into some barbed wire—which was decidedly dangerous. One fatal day I finished the course with three Russians and a fat Australian on the top of me, unintentionally making a first-class broom; first I passed over a sharp stone, and then came to a stop on the barbed wire fence. (Some of the marks caused by this episode remain with me to this day.) We had one or two nice walks weekly, on parole, escorted by a German officer.

One day, during a long walk through some pine woods, we had reached the top of a hill when we came upon a large slab of rock, about four feet thick, resting on two smaller ones, with a broad crack right through it near the centre. The German officer told us a legend about this, which affirms that at this spot somewhere about the eighth century Emperor Charlemagne met some heathen chieftain, who having already heard of his feats of strength promised to become a Christian should he be able to split this rock. The emperor took up a sledge hammer and with one tremendous blow broke the rock in two. (He must have been *some* man!)

Treatment.—When I first arrived the commandant, who was a major, was quite popular, granting all reasonable requests and not bothering us the whole time, consequently we did our best to avoid trouble; but we were in Hunland, therefore this state of affairs could not last long. The commandant was soon replaced by a colonel with a white beard and a benevolent aspect, though in reality he was inclined to be vicious and most unreasonable. He was soon followed by two junior officers, Lieutenants Briggs and Rosenthal. The former was an officer of the Reserve, one of the nicest Germans I have ever met, and I can almost safely say a gentleman. He did all that he could to avoid friction and make things run smoothly.

Rosenthal was a Regular officer and a typical Hun, who was sent round the various camps to make things generally uncomfortable for the inmates, in which capacity he was a great success. He made promises but very rarely fulfilled any, smiling to your face and at the same time arranging to have you punished. He crept along the passages in thick carpet shoes after lights out, spying on our movements, and was twice discovered listening at a keyhole to the conversation. After having been there a month I spent a fortnight in solitary confinement for my Cambrai escape, at which I cannot complain, and came out on Christmas Day. Later on, while at this camp, I carried out two sentences, each of three days, for slight offences.

Parcels and Money.—We received parcels of food and clothing from six to eight weeks after first writing for them. For the most part these came regularly, only a few being lost. This was a good thing for us, the camp authorities often providing for a meal only some raw fish and garlic or uneatable gherkins and dry black bread! Trunks, suit cases, and other heavy articles came by the American Express and were longer on their way. Parcels of food were opened, and the tins taken intact to one's individual locker, where it could be obtained most mornings at a given hour. As required the tins were then opened by the Huns and the contents placed in jars or dishes, which one must provide before it can be taken away. Sometimes whole rooms decided to mess together, sharing all their parcels, but more often two or three friends arranged their own little mess.

Letters at first came quickly, but were often delayed by the German censors at this camp, who, I believe, dealt with almost all British communications to prisoners in Germany. Money is obtained by signing a cheque, which is cashed in a week or two by the American Express. Even after America's entry into the war money could still be obtained through this company (which is, I believe, German owned). German daily papers are procurable at most camps, and usually contain a more or less intact British official *communiqué*, which is translated by some German scholar and posted up.

A map of the front is usually kept by the prisoners and corrected from time to time. Christmas was celebrated by everyone and the canteen *Weisswein* soon bought up. The Germans put an illuminated Christmas tree in the dining-hall, but unfortunately counteracted their display of good feeling by decorating the large portraits of the Kaiser and Hindenburg, who stared down at us from the walls and quite spoilt our already nasty food. On New Year's Night we collected on the stairs, and joining hands with a few French and Russians, sang "Auld Lang Syne," and scampered back to bed before the wily Huns appeared on the scene.

One day when drawing our parcels we received some little cardboard packets of compressed dates as usual, but this time a small white strip of paper was pasted on the outside of each bearing the words, "*Produce of Mesopotamia under British occupation.*" This must have been pleasant reading for the Huns. At last, one morning we were informed that in three days' time we were to proceed to an "All British" camp at Clausthal. Before our departure our Allies gave two farewell concerts in our honour, which were a great success, for when we left they knew that they were losing most of the" life" of the camp.

Living on our floor with a room to himself was a French captain of extremely doubtful character; he was a heavily built, bearded man of middle age whom nobody liked. I was told that in civil life he was a professional agitator! Now he confined his energies to making trouble between the different nationalities. He was always hanging about where he wasn't wanted, poking his nose into other people's business, and what was even more suspicious, he appeared to be on the best of terms with the Germans. He wore a long row of medals, which were inclined to change from day to day. Some senior French officers inquired if he had the right to wear them, but he refused to recognise their authority. Some Britishers had also been caught in a mysterious way just before attempting to escape.

The last night before our departure we thought we would at least show him that he was not popular. Over a dozen of us burst into his room, armed to the teeth, and holding him on to his bed covered him from head to foot with treacle, jam, coffee grounds, ashes and water, at the same time doing him no bodily injury. I expect he thought his plight more serious than it really was, for the whole place echoed with his shouts for help. Unfortunately for him the French on the floor above, being greatly pleased at the proceedings, only turned over and went to sleep again. When, after a few seconds, we bolted to our rooms he rushed down to the orderly's quarters, exclaiming," I am dying—I am covered with blood!" This sounded terrible, but when a match was struck revealing nothing but treacle and jam they could scarcely conceal their merriment.

Later on the Huns arrived and succeeded in obtaining most of our names, but even they thought the affair quite a good joke. The next morning most of the French collected quietly near the gate to give us a "send off," but the *commandant*, after screaming and being very rude to everyone had them locked in their rooms. He turned his back on us when we left, only Lieutenant Briggs having the decency to salute.

CHAPTER 6

Clausthal

It was just like house moving. The heavy luggage was sent in advance, but we preferred to carry our dearest belongings. Many of us must have resembled fully-equipped pedlars or super-caddis-worms carrying their houses on their backs, but in our case these were not composed of sticks or dead leaves, but provisions, gramophones, *mandolines*, pots, kettles, etc., tied together with string, the rattle of which appeared to amuse some of the civil population. Sometime after leaving Osnabrück the train stopped at an out-of-the-way station near Hildesheim, close to a group of men working on the line.

At once a solitary khaki-clad figure detached itself from the rest and came towards us at the run. It turned out to be a British Tommy bubbling over with pleasure at seeing some of his own race to speak to at last, after having Russians and Huns for his companions for many months. We gave him a summary of the latest news and all kinds of tinned foods. The other Russian prisoners soon followed him, looking half starved, and clamoured for bread, which we had just time to give them when a bad tempered Hun drove them back to their work.

Towards evening we passed through Hameln? (better known to us as "Hamelin"), but saw no signs of the Pied Piper. Now there was a man who was not brought into the world for nothing, but used his genius to the destruction of small Huns! The higher the train climbed into the Hartz Mountains the deeper became the snow. From the dimly-lighted carriages we could sometimes see the dark outline of high wooded hills between the snow flurries. A little before midnight we stopped with a jerk and were told to "*Aus*." As I followed the others into a restaurant winter garden affair, five minutes after our arrival, I was delighted to hear several small gramophones already playing "Bric-a-brac" and other selections from musical comedies, each insisting that its was the only tune worth listening to. Owing to the conditions escape was out of the question; the Germans did not therefore worry much—in fact, coming up in the train a rather nice N.C.O. at last yielded to my entreaties and sang a verse of the Hymn of Hate, accompanying himself on my *mandoline*.

After standing two hours in a queue at the bar I managed to procure some quite good wine which made us feel almost at home. For the rest of that night it was almost possible to imagine oneself free, but snowed up. The next morning, on hearing that the camp was about two miles away, we inquired if some of the larger suit cases might be left behind as the walking was so heavy, to be brought up later, at an extra charge, by the station sleigh, which came up to the camp every day. But we might have known that it would only be a waste of breath asking the Huns to help us in any way. (Later, when some very senior British officers arrived, bound for this camp, they received identically the same treatment.)

After an uphill struggle we reached the camp, and were kept standing quite unnecessarily for three-quarters of an hour in a snowstorm before being admitted to the dining-hall. On entering I was lucky enough to run straight into an Australian flight commander, who had often taken me up in my observing days at my first squadron, then at a village behind Ypres.

The camp is well situated, being almost surrounded by pine forests, which cover most of the Hartz Mountains. If the day is at all clear a high and rather rounded hill is visible to the eastward, conspicuous for its bleakness, standing well above the dark intervening fir-clad hills. This is the Brocken, the highest mountain in Northern Germany, on the summit of which Goethe's Faust was evolved. It is difficult to realise that it is, roughly, 5,000 feet above sea level, or the camp 2,000. The ascent in this part from the foot hills being gradual, the surrounding country is not so imposing as one would expect. Outside the camp is a small picturesque lake, which was frozen over most of the time.

On a clear evening it was fascinating to watch the superb soaring of the buzzards. It seemed as if their telescopic eyes could make out the wings on some of our tunics, for with a jeering cry they would commence gliding in a vast sweeping circle with scarcely a movement of their wings, every feather under perfect control, until at length they disappeared into the endless blue. We still have a lot to learn, but talk of the "homing instinct," if only a few aeroplanes had been handy I know which would have made the quickest non-stop flight to "Blighty."

The next day a number of Belgian officers left to take up their abode in the quarters vacated by us in Osnabrück, many of them resplendent in their tasselled caps, and a few wearing clanking swords which they had been allowed to retain in recognition of the gallant way they had defended some of the Liège and Antwerp forts. With them went two Belgian officers, who, curiously enough, could not speak their lingo. This was not surprising, however, as their real names were Captain Nicholl, R.F.C., and Lieutenant Reid, R.N. It appeared they intended to jump the train before reaching their destination and have a try for the Dutch border. German trains often go slowly and stop, but as luck would have it this one, as we afterwards heard, refused to do anything of the sort.

Whether Captain Nicholl succeeded in getting off I do not know, but Lieutenant Reid, seeing discovery imminent, jumped through the carriage window and broke his ankles. They were both taken to Osnabrück and Nicholl was sent back under arrest. After three weeks Lieutenant Reid returned, lame, but quite cheery. As he was under arrest, however, we could not learn much of their treatment, though it was common knowledge that he had left hospital *very* soon, and was made to walk up from the station as best he could. His sentence was lengthened by some days on the charge of answering his wrong name at a roll call on arrival at Osnabrück, but as he was quite unable to stand this was obviously a fabrication.

When we had been there about ten days a lot more British officers arrived from Friedburg, where they had received quite good treatment. Many of the prisoners at this camp had been taken at Mons, La Cateau and Ypres, and were consequently a little out of date. They could hardly realise what a "Somme barrage" was like, and were therefore known as the "Bow and Arrow" men! On the journey to Clausthal two of them managed to jump from the train and got clear away. About this time five Italian officers were warned to leave the next day. The preceding night, after supper, Colonel Bond (K.O.Y.L.I.), after a short speech, proposed the toast "*Viva Italia*," which we drank in canteen *Weisswein*, or imitation port, to which a senior Italian officer enthusiastically replied with a "*Viva Inghilterra*." After their departure the camp contained British only, the remaining number of officers being a little over three hundred.

Accommodation.—The principal building, in which about half of us lived, was a *Kurhaus*, or small hydro, in peace time, with a large dining-hall at one end. The smallest bedrooms were occupied by one or two senior officers, while the remainder held about half a dozen. A shower-bath was on the premises. The rest of us were quartered in three temporary wooden barracks, where most of the rooms were rather over-crowded, holding from six to eight fellows.

Recreation.—At a portion of the grounds was a fairly steep incline and on this we made a short toboggan run, banking the snow up steeply at the turn to avoid going through the barbed wire. In many instances it must have been amusing to watch a small sleigh being steered by a novice, with fat individuals sitting on the top of him, trying to avoid the young trees, usually without any success. Unfortunately for me I had a nasty knack of always being in the worst crashes. It is impossible to find a more effective way of destroying boots than continually steering with one's feet. Other people displayed their extensive knowledge of winter sports by skiing, or rather lying on their backs, unintentionally waving their skis in the air. This soon had to be abandoned, however, as the weather soon became uncertain, often changing from a hard frost to a violent thaw every two or three days.

A naval officer in my barrack received a miniature billiard-table, which became immensely popular. Cards, roulette, ping-pong and chess greatly assisted in passing the time. We also had quite a good camp library, the books mostly having been received from home. I often heard it remarked that life there was one long queue, and it was not far wrong. Often one passed the morning waiting one's turn for the "tin room," or newly arrived parcels, while soon after lunch it was customary to see the more patient individuals already lining up chairs and settling down to their books, to wait for hot water which was sold at tea time. All this may sound most enjoyable, but I will now endeavour to explain a little of the wonderful system then in vogue at this camp, the only object of which seemed to be to remind you in an objectionable manner that you were a prisoner on every possible occasion.

Treatment.—When we first arrived the commandant was not so bad, but after several visits from corps headquarters at Hanover, he resigned his post, it is said, on the grounds that he could not treat British officers like common criminals, as he was supposed to. I think this is highly probable, though I cannot vouch for the truth of the assertion, it being only hearsay. He was replaced by a fat and rather harmless dugout captain, who proved to be only a pompous figurehead. The camp was entirely run by the second in command, Lieutenant Wolfe. In

England persons of this type are so rarely met with that our language does not contain the necessary words to describe them adequately. In Germany they are comparatively common, therefore, collectively they may be put down as belonging to the "super-swine class!"! Wolfe was arrogance personified. He possessed a closely-cropped bullet head, and a round, somewhat bloated pale face, near the centre of which gleamed two small, cold, calculating blue eyes; the whole effect so strongly resembled a white pig that among ourselves he was usually known as "pig face." He belonged to a reserve Hanoverian regiment, and was a schoolmaster by profession. It is small wonder that children under such authority never learn to know the true meaning of the word "*kultur.*" Somehow he knew about the treacling affair at our last camp, for after getting our names from Osnabrück, he strained every nerve to get us court-martialled and punished.

Two or three times a week we criminals had to assemble outside his room at an appointed hour. After a long wait "My Lord" strolled in, usually an hour late, walking very slowly, chewing a cigar. At first he only produced a small packet of papers, on most of which our individual statements were written, and asked absurd questions through an interpreter. But as time went on the case assumed larger proportions, and the bundle of nonsense increased to an enormous size. At almost every visit we had to sign some new document certifying that we understood the latest communication on the subject from headquarters. After much hard work "pig face" achieved his object, and we were warned to attend a court-martial at Hanover. However, this is worthy of a separate chapter.

One day an impossible staff captain arrived from Hanover to inspect the camp. He was a large, arrogant bully, who brought with him two detectives for the purpose of searching our rooms and kit for forbidden articles. We will not waste time discussing his manners; he had none. The detectives seemed quite decent, and therefore cannot have been properly dehumanised by the powers that be. In German camps it is forbidden to sit or lie on one's bed during the day, unless one has reported sick at roll call. This captain suddenly entered a room in our barrack and surprised a Scotsman lying on his bed reading a book. Seeing that the culprit had his clothes on, he screamed out such a stream of unintelligible curses and threats, that had a similar noise taken place at the zoo, I am sure the keepers would have rushed out to stop the monkey fight. The Scotsman waited until this torrent had somewhat abated, then slowly getting to his feet, he drawled out in a bewildered way, "And how's your faither!" It is doubtful whether the startled captain understood this kind inquiry or not, but he rushed out of the room and, grabbing a sentry's bayonet, returned and stuck it in the boards at his feet.

Ours was the next room he favoured. Without the semblance of a knock he burst in, and as nothing of importance had been found during the search, swaggered up and down in a most offensive manner with his nose in the air. In a few seconds he came to a stop beside me and shouted that he wished me to stand to attention, half dressed as I was (having just been searched). This was just about the limit, so pretending not to understand what he meant I turned round and busied myself with my clothing, at the same time humming softly to myself the air of "Pack up your troubles," to relieve my feelings and stifle a desire to give him one under the jaw. On a word of command two scared sentries appeared, having been ordered to take me to the guardroom immediately.

The usually harmless *commandant* was so frightened that he rolled his eyes and screamed after me, when exhaustion put an end to the captain's song. It was pitiable to see two such men possessing not an atom of self-control between them, but it was not so amusing as one might think. It certainly looked as if I should be murdered without delay. I was put into a room adjoining that occupied by the main guard, where I remained for three hours. During this period I got into conversation with some of the soldiers and was surprised at the bitter way they spoke of Lieutenant Wolfe, so much so that if he returned to the front I should be inclined to think that the quarter where his greatest danger lay was not in front but behind.

When I had the room to myself I spent the time exploring for useful articles. My oft-interrupted search resulted in the discovery of a heap of things in the far corner. At length an officer arrived and informed me that I should only receive three days' "*stuben*"—arrest (solitary confinement). After which I was released. On re-entering the camp I did my best to look innocent, though, as luck would have it, I was really the richer by a couple of maps, a compass and some candles! One of the orderlies in the camp was a cobbler, but though the Huns frequently assured us they would provide him with the necessary tools, it took two months for their promise to materialise.

During this period my already patched boots threatened to give out altogether. I wrote a note to the *commandant*, explaining that I was daily expecting boots from England, but as these appeared to have been delayed, asked that I might be allowed to order some canvas shoes at the canteen in the meantime. The next day the interpreter handed me the answer: "*Order leather from England, and have the boots resoled.*" I could not help smiling, and casually remarked that it was worse than useless. Whereupon he snapped, "What, you say that the *commandant's* note is useless? All right, I will you report."

In due course the usual notice was posted up to the effect "That the English *Ober*-Lieutenant Gerald Knight would for gross insolence the next three days in arrest spend." Usually, roll call took place outside the main building, and as it generally meant standing in water or melting snow, was not particularly pleasant. Wolfe very often managed to take these parades, and did not miss this excellent opportunity for showing his authority. After arriving late he would stroll up and down the line, hands in pockets, looking as dignified as possible, always wasting time. "*Appel*," when properly conducted, never lasted more than ten minutes or a quarter of an hour.

On one occasion, Wolfe, who was well protected against the cold, kept us standing in a blizzard for an hour and a half, during which time he counted us five or six times, obviously for his own amusement. It was bad enough to have to stand there oneself, but it was much more annoying to watch our senior officers, majors, colonels, and a major-general, awaiting the pleasure of a conceited German lieutenant. Almost every day some new order was issued, for the most part affecting little things, for example—stating that in future no food would be allowed in the rooms.

A few days later it was not allowed in the cupboards standing in the passages. Soon it was only allowed in the dining-hall, where the accommodation was quite inadequate. One day two fellows were quietly walking down a path near the wire, when a sentry raised his rifle and threatened to shoot them if they did not at once go further from the wire! They refused to move, and told the sentry that they had a perfect right there. Whereupon the man at last lowered his rifle. On a complaint being made, Lieutenant Wolfe, knowing that few people were about, ingeniously squashed the case by refusing to take the matter up unless six witnesses were produced.

There was a second lieutenant, junior to Wolfe (commonly known as the Worm!), who arrived after receiving promotion from the ranks. He was rather a miserable sort of person, inclined to follow Wolfe's example in most things. He was forever on the prowl and it never occurred to him to knock before entering a room. Once he came into our room and, assisted by two guards, removed the mirror, shaving tackle, hair brushes, etc., from the window, placing them on the wash-hand stand in the darkest corner of the room. After this performance he drew himself up sedately and exclaimed," That is the way we do things in Germany!" These little incidents are most annoying at any time, but especially so when one is wearing boots possessing good kicking qualities.

It was not until May that the snow finally disappeared and we were treated to a spell of warm weather, during which everyone did their best to get sunburnt, and set to work on the new tennis court we had permission to make.

Lizards and frogs appeared from nowhere and endeavoured to inform us that spring was approaching. It is curious the way camp life again makes one childish and easily amused. For instance, it was quite a common occurrence to see a small crowd of fellows looking excitedly at something. On closer investigation it in most cases turned out to be a toad or a worm. As it became dry underfoot we were able to go out for walks on parole with a German officer. The stout commandant usually took us, and not only did he make himself quite agreeable, but also chose some very pretty paths among the various pine woods. One afternoon two fellows succeeded in cutting the outside wire in broad daylight and getting into the woods unobserved.

Seeing his opportunity a tall Canadian, named Colquhoun, hastily gathered up his valuables and dived through the inviting gap in the wire (which had been cleverly cut behind some young fir trees and up beside a post). He was just disappearing into the woods at record speed (the sentry's back being still turned) when he was seen by some children playing on a hillock a little way off. They at once made a noise, and several of them rushed down to tell the sentry. That man, however, was much too grand to listen to "kids" talking nonsense, so drove them off with many threats and violent gestures. When the escape was discovered, green-uniformed soldiers of *Jaeger* regiments and mounted foresters scoured the woods for nearly two days without any success. Shortly after a notice was posted up stating that when the escaped officers were recaptured, they would in all probability be tried by court-martial for breaking their parole in looking for hiding places when out for walks; this, needless to say, was all nonsense, the officers in question being miles away by that time.

This notice could not be regarded in any other light than that of an insult to British officers in general, causing much resentment.

All future walks were voluntarily given up, and at evening "*appel*" all parole cards, without exception, were returned to the Huns by mutual consent, to avoid any insinuations of this sort in the future. After being out for about a fortnight the outlaws were all recaptured and taken to Ströhen, where I afterwards met them. The first two put up a very good show, being recaptured in an exhausted condition by a road guard, twenty odd kilometres from the frontier, much to their disgust.

My friend, the Canadian, fought a good fight against an unkind fate. While washing in a stream one night he was taken by a man with a revolver looking for an escaped Russian prisoner. He was then put into prison at a men's camp, where he succeeded in obtaining some wire-cutters from other Britishers. Forcing his way through the sky-light into a dark and rainy night, he dropped to earth, cut the wire and was again free. The drop previous to cutting the wire had, however, damaged his compass, which stuck and led him south instead of west.

Three days later he was taken near a bridge over a river by men and trained dogs, and transferred to a town prison. There I believe he received quite decent food, for which he was very thankful. During the late afternoon some children came to annoy him by shouting rude remarks from the passage. Even these little wretches were of some use, for at their departure they touched something on the outside of his door which jingled, and turned out to be a bunch of keys, which he was able to get possession of by pulling them through the sliding panel used by the guard for spying on the prisoner. When it was dark the adventurer produced the keys and by dint of much labour succeeded in opening his own cell and walking out.

At the back of one of the nearer buildings he discovered a bicycle, which he appropriated without a second thought. Having discovered his whereabouts he struck north to get into his original line, and was unfortunately discovered by some N.C.O.'s the next day in almost a starving condition repairing his bicycle in a shed. After such an attempt as this it is indeed hard to return to serve one's sentence at a camp prison or fortress, knowing full well that, although having done one's utmost, even the slightest official recognition is out of the question.

After the second escape the Hun in charge of the men's camp 'phoned to Clausthal, stating that the officer had been recaptured. Wolfe hearing the joyous news started out to bring back the truant as a lesson to others. "*But when he got there the cupboard was bare,*" so he

129

returned to the "*Hartz-Gebirge*" empty-handed and disconsolate. The only really decent German at the camp appeared to be an "*aspirant*," or first class warrant officer, who treated us quite fairly when opportunity offered; however, his superiors saw to it that this was not often.

Parcels.—These arrived fairly well, but were periodically hoarded up by the Huns for a week or ten days, where we could not get them without any previous warning. When drawing food all the tins had to be left behind until wanted for immediate consumption. It was therefore very difficult to lay in a supply against such emergencies. During these periods most messes determined, if possible, to have a meal of sorts at teatime. Gradually, as the provisions got lower and lower, the menu read somewhat as follows: Tea (no milk or sugar); very limited black bread, thinly spread with soup essence, or *café au lait* (when the dripping, lard or potted meat had finally vanished). The meal itself was rather nauseating, but afterwards it was most gratifying to be able to say that you had had tea! When this playful little "strafe" was removed by an order from Hanover the accumulated parcels nearly caused the death of the Germans working in the distributing room.

Letters were very slow in arriving. Once a general, while inspecting the camp, entered the parcel room, where he saw an English captain assisting with the sorting of the parcels. On finding that he spoke German well the general advised him to devote his spare time to the further study of that language, which he said would be very useful to him later. The captain was notorious for saying exactly what he thought, and be hanged to the consequences. His reply must have been more than the German bargained for: "Sir, I do not intend to waste my time learning a dead language!" It is probable that the general had had previous dealings with the British, and therefore possessed a sense of humour so rare to the Teuton, for he passed on without awarding the expected punishment.

CHAPTER 7

Court-Martialled! and Proud of It, Too!

It is not usual to boast of the fact that one has been court-martialled, but I would not have missed this experience for anything. Early in the morning of May 15th, 1917, we twelve gaol-birds, after being carefully searched, left for the station escorted by eight guards. During the march I began softly humming a tune, but was at once silenced by an angry sentry, who told me that no noise of any sort was allowed. Turning to the N.C.O. I remarked that although he appeared to be in charge of the party he had not objected to my behaviour, and added that this seemed almost as if the private was exceeding his duty. This appealed to the dignity of his position, and although he evidently did not like me, he told the sentry off. On reaching the station we had an unpleasant surprise, for there, awaiting us on the platform, was our old friend, Wolfe.

In the early afternoon we got out of the train at a small station and were told that we should have to wait some hours for the connection. The senior member of our party inquired whether it was possible to get anything to eat, as it was already very late for the midday meal. Wolfe said he would try and led us into the restaurant, where a waiter inquired if we would have white or green beans. These dishes sounded so tempting that we ordered mixed. When the result was served (beans stewed with gravy and a little potato), it certainly greatly exceeded our expectations, being really appetising. When this was finished a resourceful member of the party produced some cards, and poker became the order of the day. The game was still in progress when one of the others called our attention to the Red Cross collecting box on the table. In trying to decipher the appeal for subscriptions for the

131

wounded, he had made a great discovery. Actually beside the red cross in a small circle made by a rubber stamp were the words, "*Gott strafe England!*"

Naturally, this display of childishness amused us greatly, creating a general laugh. This frivolity in the face of a court-martial was more than Wolfe could stand, so after one withering glance in our direction he turned his back on us and stalked majestically from the room. Luckily I had in my possession a good supply of tin canteen money (which was valueless outside the camp); this was at once transferred to the box as quickly as possible. It isn't often that an Englishman has the pleasure of subscribing to his own special hate box! I am simply longing to know if the money was eventually returned to the camp for its equivalent value. Should this book in the near future be read in Germany, as I expect it will, would some kind Hun take the trouble to satisfy my curiosity? "Royal Air Force, England," will always find me.

About six o'clock that evening we reached Hanover and were marched off through some of the main streets to an unknown destination. The town is all right; it is the people that spoil it. Proceeding down some broad streets we passed some very fine buildings, statues and fountains. Once a well-dressed woman unintentionally crossed our path, with the result that a sentry roughly threw her aside without a word of apology. Passing through a small park we halted before a low, dirty-looking stone building, with every window strongly barred.

Presently Lieutenant Wolfe emerged with a smile of welcome and bade us enter. In a small courtyard a German N.C.O., with a loud rasping voice, ordered the prison guard to take us to our quarters. After much jangling of keys we were separated, to our amazement, and each one of the party locked in a cell by himself. Near the ceiling was one small window about two feet square. On examination this exit proved to be guarded with fine wire netting and thick iron bars firmly embedded in cement. As usual, there was a special spy-hole in the door which had to be covered on the inside. Attached to each end of the bed were two strong shackles, evidently intended to fasten the occupant down if necessary. We afterwards learnt that this was the garrison prison, it being considerably worse than the civil one. It does not seem surprising that they are able to maintain their iron discipline, if they resort to these methods.

I think the reader will agree that this is hardly a fit place to lodge officers who, as yet, were only awaiting their trial. Several times I faintly heard the whirring of aeroplanes outside, but only managed to see one by pulling myself up to the window. We relieved the monotony a little by whistling to each other in the Morse code what we thought of the Huns for putting us there. The thickness of the walls, however, soon put a stop to this. During the night I was awakened by several thuds, followed by a crash, which came from somewhere overhead. This puzzled me at the time, but the next day I found the noise had been caused by one of our party rat-hunting with the aid of a boot which had landed on a tin basin instead of the rat.

The next morning the man with a voice like a nutmeg grater released us from our cells, and after a few preliminaries we were marched off across the square to a large building, which we entered about ten o'clock. Then ensued a long but interesting wait, during which we watched all sorts and conditions of Huns passing up and down the main staircase. Amongst them we saw several colonels, a general and a very smart monocled major, whose helmet was rather the shape of a fireman's, showing that he was in some crack cavalry regiment— dragoons, I think. They mostly wore pale blue-grey overcoats, and their buttons, sword-hilts and golden eagles on their helmets glittered exquisitely. The general appearance was smart enough, but everything seemed a trifle overdone, giving one the impression that they had just stepped out of a bandbox.

Had a British officer been standing beside these Germans, wearing his sword, the contrast would have been a strange one, for while looking just as smart the uniform would have had the appearance of being infinitely more serviceable. There passed quite a number of Hun privates with downcast eyes, having just received their long sentences. An interpreter having nothing to do, tried hard to prove to us that the U-boats would very soon bring England to her knees, but gave up the attempt on receiving an invitation to the camp to watch the daily arrival of the over-laden parcel cart.

Eventually we were ushered into the court, bareheaded, trying very hard to look meek. The opening questions and formalities took up a lot of time, and it really was a terrible strain trying not to laugh when the interpreter solemnly explained to a German captain that one of our party belonged to the *Middlesex* Regiment. Before getting to business our individual conduct sheets were read out, mine being about as black as it could be. At our request two French majors from Osnabrück were present. Both spoke well on our behalf, explaining that this could only be a quarrel between the French and British in any case, but that they were delighted at what had occurred, and most certainly did not wish to prosecute. Everything went in our favour, and, when the treacling was described, even the presiding Hun general laughed. The public prosecutor, as usual, asked for the maximum punishment, 600 *marks* fine or 100 days fortress. Whereupon the court rose and left the room, looking justice itself.

On their return it was announced that the junior three of our party, who had not actually entered the Frenchman's room, were let off with a caution, and that all the rest were each fined five hundred *marks*, or fifty days in a fortress. This showed how they wanted our money; of course the whole thing had been arranged beforehand. On inquiring what the money would go to support we were told that it would probably be the war loan. A few minutes later, after leaving in a rebellious mood, we were lucky enough to meet the two Frenchmen, from whom we learnt that they too had spent the night in cells in the same prison. Later on I was given to understand that before a subsequent court-martial two British officers spent the night on a sort of mattress in a corner of the guardroom.

The return journey was accomplished without incident, except for an attempt on our part to speak to a captured guardsman, who was loading trucks, which was promptly squashed by Wolfe snapping out *"Das geht nicht."* Nevertheless, a tin or two of food found its way out of the window.

The weather at Clausthal, after a brief interval of snowstorms, became beautifully warm, and the prospect of spending the summer in the Hartz Mountains was almost alluring. About this time General Friedrichs (in charge of prisoners of war) made a speech in the Reichstag, in the course of which he stated that the English treated their prisoners better than any other nation (or so the translation read), and went on to say that in return English prisoners must receive good treatment, so that at the conclusion of hostilities they would take back good remembrances of Germany to their own country. In my case things certainly did change (I expect as a result of the speech)—for the worse. A week later thirty-five officers, including myself, were sent to Ströhen, a camp which will certainly be remembered long after peace is declared, but I doubt if the memory will be a pleasant one.

CHAPTER 8

Ströhen

Previous to our departure Wolfe personally searched our belongings. Although a long journey lay in front of us, he only allowed each individual to carry two small tins of food. In reply to our protests he said that, as things were always well arranged in Germany, our luggage would therefore arrive at the same time as ourselves. This was, of course, absolutely untrue, but we had to submit. During the great search Wolfe, seeing that I was wearing a belt made of plaited string (Yes, Mr. Wolfe, the belt in question was made of blind cord cut from the *kurhaus* windows!), and noting that it was something unusual, ordered me to leave it behind. Taking it off, I politely handed it to him, and expressed my hope that he would keep it as a souvenir! With a charming smile he replied, "Three days *stuben* arrest," which I acknowledged with a bow.

Outside the camp, on our way to the station we looked back and saw the roll call was in progress. Thereupon we gave three cheers for the many friends we were leaving behind us, in spite of the fact that Wolfe and the commandant were on parade. We travelled second class and at one station were even allowed to buy beer; our guards were quite reasonable, and things in general went off pleasantly. We stayed some time at an out-of-the-way station east of Osnabrück, where quite a crowd of children collected. They scrambled excitedly for the sweets and cigarettes which we threw them. Arriving at a little station called Ströhen, which seemed to be on a large moor, we got out and started for the camp, the German officer bringing up the rear in a victoria. After ten minutes' walking down a lonely road we made out a group of low wooden huts surrounded by high arc lamps and wire, on a desolate moorland. Surely this could not be our destination, the good camp we had been led to expect.

But after inquiring our guards told us it was, although they were nearly as much surprised at its appearance as we were. At all events we were determined to hide our feelings and look cheery. Quickening our pace we approached the camp singing the almost forgotten song, "Tipperary," were marched through the gates, and halted in front of a small group of German officers, in the centre of the camp. We at once distinguished the commandant, a major, with a first class iron cross hanging from his collar. He was rather short and stout with a square face; his grey whiskers terminated in a small double-pointed beard; this completed his "Hunnish" appearance! With his hands behind his back he welcomed us with a sullen stare, all the while puffing stolidly at his cigar. Had the Huns rehearsed this scene for a week they could not have given us a more heathen reception.

No one even made a show at politeness by a nod or a salute. A stout and ugly sergeant-major (named Muller), wearing a gaudy blue and red uniform and sword, bawled at us to dress by the right, as if he were addressing a squad of recruits. He very nearly exploded when we ignored his insolent words of command. A rather common little interpreter commenced calling the roll, beginning with a captain, but only shouting his surname, to which there was no response. When his voice gradually rose to a shriek the Englishman stepped out and said, "I suppose you mean Captain so-and-so." The interpreter explained matters to the commandant, who must have realised that they were in the wrong, for in future we were addressed by our proper rank. (Victory No. 1.)

We were each given a disc, on which was stamped our camp number (mine is now residing at home), and shown into our rooms. Late that night about two hundred fellows arrived from Crefeld, and Muller, finding he could not intimidate them, made such a noise that he was "choked off" by the *commandant*. We learnt that this place had been built as a Russian reprisal camp, but that lately Roumanian officers had been confined there. We were the first British these people had ever had to deal with. Hence their very bad manners!

Now in a camp of this sort it is very necessary to stand up for one's rights when treated unfairly, otherwise the Germans soon forget that you have any rights; at the same time, if the treatment is fair, one does one's best to avoid friction. The best instance of a result of the former treatment occurred the next afternoon. When some of the Crefeld party, who had been allowed to bring provisions with them, found that it was not possible to obtain hot water for making tea, some inventive person at once started a little fire of sticks outside my room. Almost immediately a N.C.O. leading half a dozen armed men appeared on the scene and told the offender in a dreadful voice to put the fire out at once. Instead of complying the culprit dodged into a barrack and out of a window on the opposite side and disappeared. When the Huns were able to comprehend the audacity of this move they had to put the fire out themselves.

Half an hour later a sentry, seeing three fires burning in the same place, strolled over and quietly informed those concerned that fires were not allowed, and that unless they were put out he would have to make a report to the *commandant*. The result was that they were at once extinguished with the aid of sand. Our baggage did not arrive for nearly a week; then, instead of being given out, it was locked up for another five days before we received it all. During this time we had to live on the German food as best we could.

Accommodation.—Our quarters consisted of three long and two smaller badly made huts, divided into rooms containing, mostly, two or six officers. The mattresses were mostly dirty and hard, being stuffed with paper and cardboard, which formed sharp edges and lumps. The first week about ten of us found "creepy crawlies," and shortly before our departure I succeeded in attracting some while in the camp hospital! The Huns provided us with the German equivalent for" Keating's" after much agitation, after making us pay for it. The doctor said that the newly captured prisoners must have brought the creatures into the camp. That may have been true in a few cases, but even so they are to blame for not making adequate arrangements to prevent it. We each received a tin basin, but the washing was all done at three pumps outside.

All the drinking water was derived from this source, and had a strong and disagreeable taste. A few feet away from each pump was a stagnant pool into which the waste water flowed. I think it is reasonable to suppose that a good proportion of it, after filtering through the sand, was pumped up again. In spite of these trifles we were told that the water had been analysed and passed by the medical authorities. I suppose both the colour and flavour were only due to the presence of iron, in which case I have no doubt it was an excellent tonic. I should have liked to have seen the doctor's face had he been made to swallow a glassful. I am thinking of forming a company for the purpose of building a hydro on the site of the old camp, so that everyone may have an opportunity of enjoying perfect health by taking the Ströhen waters. I hope the reader will assist me by buying shares in this excellent concern. (A large cemetery will, of course, be necessary, but grave-digging should not prove to be expensive, the soil being very light!)

The safest and most comfortable place in the camp was the small hospital, which was under the care of a very decent corporal in a Brandenburg regiment. The dining and common rooms were in one long barrack, divided into two sections. At one end of the latter was a canteen of sorts, which ultimately improved considerably. The sanitary arrangements were most primitive, the breezes constantly reminding one of their inefficiency. For the first month the weather was glorious, and during the evening stroll round it was maddening to watch the red sun slowly sinking behind the distant woods to the westward, showing us the way to Holland and freedom. The journey by train would have been accomplished in a few hours under ordinary circumstances. It was almost incredible to think, though it was only too true, that a few strands of wire and some grey-clad sentries could keep us confined in this desert-like camp, containing neither grass nor trees, isolated from all the pleasures of summer.

Whenever there was a wind we enjoyed a whirling sandstorm. Often I have seen it so thick as to temporarily obscure the further camp buildings. If we had only been allowed camels and facilities for exercising, we should soon have looked upon a journey across the Sahara as mere child's play. After a victory (real or imaginary), or an anniversary, it was with very rebellious feelings that we watched the German flag fluttering in the breezes. I did not mind the coloured one quite so much, but it was almost more than I could stand to see the pale yellow flag, framing the treacherous scraggy black eagle, flying over my head. In one part of the camp there was just room for a game of tennis. Several classes were formed for learning languages, and indulging in "physical jerks" (culture), though I'm sorry to say I much preferred watching and jeering with the ever increasing majority.

Occasionally sports days were organised, which went off in style, the chief items being short races, jumping, cock-fighting, also a competition which necessitated each individual eating a sticky bun dangling from a tightly stretched string without using his hands. This may not sound much of a feat, but when one realises that the bun consists of a chunk of stale black bread exuding coarse treacle, the difficulty will be better understood. Several canaries had been brought along from the former camp. In one instance a man in the Flying Corps, possessing a sitting bird, carried her so carefully that she never left the eggs and eventually reared her young at Ströhen.

Latterly chip carving became the fashion, as it was then possible to obtain the necessary articles from a German firm through the canteen. Concerts were frequently held, and as the camp contained very considerable talent, we had some really first class performances, after being allowed to hire a piano from the nearest town. One day a new lot of orderlies arrived and took up their quarters in a barrack separated from our part of the camp by some wire. Among their number was a private called Cheeseman, a born comedian, who used to get up sing-songs and sketches; the star turn, however, was a selection from his orchestra, which he used to conduct with a broomstick from an inverted bucket. The instruments were two *mandolines*, one banjo, one *mandola*, a tin whistle, an accordion, a rattle, a comb, and a lump of iron. Somehow the performers played in tune, but they always sent us into fits of laughter, and even amused the watching Huns.

Although Cheeseman often disappeared into cells for several days, he was never really squashed and always reappeared with a new joke. I was lucky enough to receive a good assortment of flower seeds from home, including sunflowers, sweet peas, nasturtiums, etc.; these I immediately planted in a tiny museum-like garden, and tended carefully, in the hope that someday the plants would assume large enough proportions to enable me to believe temporarily on special occasions that I was actually amid the flowers of good old England. In my case the deception was fortunately not necessary, as I was destined to enjoy the real thing, though unfortunately in hospital.

Treatment.—The first roll calls, though unnecessarily long, were quite entertaining. They were conducted by a guards lieutenant with a pronounced limp, who went by the name of "Cork-leg." Even when speaking of a matter of no importance his voice would become louder and louder until it threatened to reach a shrill scream. On one occasion when the interpreter was not present, some unoffending person asked the Hun a question in English. Cork-leg replied, with a dreadful roar, that we must understand that the language of the camp was German, and German only. Things were going a little too far, so every time the gentleman gave expression to his thoughts in too vehement a manner most of us whispered a long-drawn "Hush." The parade being in square formation, when he turned suddenly to arrest the offender, he found those facing him wearing an air of injured innocence, while those in his rear continued the good work. This had the desired effect, and although it meant *"stuben* arrest" for several fellows, the officer soon realised what an ass he was making of himself and became almost normal, with the result that things went smoothly for a while.

Soon after our arrival, a fortnight, to be correct, the newly captured infantry officers, numbering about fifty, were ordered to give up their steel helmets at a given roll call. This naturally went against the grain. The owners mostly destroyed the rubber padding and hid the helmets, resolving that at least they should not benefit the Hun. At the appointed time eight instead of fifty were surrendered to the officer on duty. On the morning of the twelfth of June a number of German soldiers set to work with poles and hooks to drag the pools for submerged helmets. By and by they succeeded in picking out quite a number of those steel fish, every additional one landed calling forth a subdued cheer from the onlookers. In the afternoon, having nothing to do but kill time, I strolled out of a barrack, my hands in my pockets, with no immediate objective in view.

Outside a few Germans were still fishing for helmets, while half a dozen Britishers were lazily watching operations. After joining them for a minute or two I turned to walk over to another building. True, there were some sentries with fixed bayonets lounging about, but that was nothing unusual, for they might well be in charge of the orderlies who were working nearby. I had not gone ten yards when a tall, unshaven *Landsturmer* swung round and barred my way. He told me with a snarl that I was not allowed there and motioned me back with his hand. I told him that I was not aware of any new order and only wished to go to the neighbouring building. Whereupon he repeated his words in a still more offensive tone, and brought his rifle to the ready. (Even a German sentry is supposed to be reasonably polite when addressing an officer prisoner for the first time, but this man was purposely rude.) I replied that if he addressed me as a British officer and not as a dog I should obey him at once, otherwise I should remain where I was.

After a few more unintelligible threats he advanced, brandishing his weapon, at which I turned sideways to call to a German N.C.O. and protest against such treatment. The kindly sentry aimed a smashing blow at my left foot, which I was luckily able to partially deflect by a slight movement of my knee. Things were certainly quite disturbing, for the next instant he stuck the bayonet almost through my right thigh. The proceeding was not particularly pleasant, feeling very like a sharp burn, but I was almost too surprised to realise fully what had happened, so consequently remained standing where I was. Vaguely I realised that the sentry had withdrawn his bayonet for another thrust, this time evidently intended to enter my body. Glancing down I saw that my trouser leg was saturated and streaming with blood, which was even welling out of my shoe on to the ground, showing that an artery had been severed.

Not being particularly partial to bayonet thrusts, I decided that I could now abandon my argument without loss of prestige. I succeeded in hobbling a few yards to the rear, at the same time holding the artery above the wound in an endeavour to check the flow of blood. This, however, did not prove very successful, the sand continuing to turn red behind me. Just as I was in the act of falling, a number of our fellows, seeing what had happened, rushed up and carried me hastily into the camp hospital, where a tourniquet was applied and the doctor sent for. The time was then a quarter-past three, and the doctor did not arrive till after seven o'clock. I rather fancy if an accident of that sort had occurred in an English prison camp containing over four hundred German officers, it would not be necessary to wait almost four hours before the arrival of a qualified doctor.

At the best of times a very tight tourniquet is distinctly uncomfortable. The medical orderly thinking that I should lose consciousness and seeing the *commandant* enter the room, explained the circumstances and asked if he might give me a little brandy. After due consideration and much chewing at the ragged end of his eternal cigar, he replied that as water would be given to a wounded German soldier, it was good enough for me. Though I pretended not to hear, these remarks impressed me considerably. The N.C.O. looked after me very well, and early next morning took me to the station in an ambulance on my way to Hanover Hospital. Two private soldiers acted as stretcher-bearers, with the N.C.O. in charge.

When the train arrived it was found that the stretcher was too broad to go into a carriage, so I travelled in the luggage van, among trunks, bicycles and baskets of fish. The Germans were quite jolly and sang a few songs, while I, in a half dead condition, endeavoured to accompany them on my beloved *mandoline*. At Hanover I was dumped down at a Red Cross centre below the station to await the ambulance. Soon quite a pretty nurse (for a wonder) came up and inquired if I was English. I could not resist replying in German: "Yes, sister, I am one of those *Schweinhund Englanders!*"

To my surprise she seemed quite embarrassed, and hastily answered me that they did not say that *now*. (Emphasis on the *now*.) In the conveyance I lay beside a wounded German private, also bound for hospital. When my curiosity had broken the ice, he told me that he had just returned from the Messines Ridge, where he had acquired a great respect for British artillery and mines (though he himself was a sapper).

The Hanover hospitals which usually take in prisoners are Nos. 1 and 7; to my relief I was taken to No. 1, which is recognised as the best. I received practically the same treatment as the German patients, and occupied a room with three other British officers. Some of the food we received was quite good, a little fresh milk and butter, and one or two whitish rolls of bread, and, of course, the usual doubtful soups. Immediately outside the window was a large flowering acacia tree, looking delightfully shady and cool after Ströhen desert. Another luxury we sometimes enjoyed was strawberries, which the German orderly bought in large quantities, afterwards selling them to some of the doctors and nurses as well as ourselves.

At frequent intervals a band outside played a very ordinary uninteresting dead march, announcing each time a German (usually a patient) had gone "West." Soon after my arrival I saw a Zeppelin flying very low over the town. I was delighted and remarked to a Bosch that it was the first Zeppelin I had ever seen. He was quite indignant and told me that I ought to know that it was a Schutte-Lanz, a new type of airship. My education must have been sadly neglected!

Bayonet wounds are, for several reasons, liable to become septic; mine, however, healed up remarkably quickly, saving me endless bother. In a fortnight I started back to the camp, accompanied by a N.C.O. and a private, who helped me slowly along. We went by train, without causing much interest. This was a good thing, for it is very hard to look dignified when feeling like nothing on earth, and looking as white as a sheet. Many of the small boys were dressed up as soldiers in one way or another, and I twice saw a small ragamuffin band with tins for kettle-drums. Just wouldn't there be a fine scrap if a similar band of London children had suddenly rounded the corner! Personally, I would back the cockney spirit against any other.

This was my second visit to Hanover, and on no occasion had I seen a motor other than the one ambulance car, though I heard two in the distance. Owing to the scarcity of rubber I was surprised at the number of bicycles present in the streets, but closer inspection proved that that difficulty had been overcome by a clever invention, by which the shock is lessened by an outer wooden rim held in position by strong springs, which are compressed as they take the weight. During the train journey my escort, as usual, drew my attention to the splendid way in which the Germans treated their prisoners by allowing them to travel second class. They simply would not believe that German officers in England always travelled first. The private, who owned a cigar factory in Hanover, became quite chatty and seemed very anxious to know if I thought the trade relationships between England and Germany would be the same as ever after the war. He was very surprised and, indeed, quite distressed when I told him that I thought there would be a considerable change—it seemed that the idea had never occurred to him before.

I was not sorry when the camp was reached and I entered the little camp hospital to remain there for another two weeks. Several fellows having escaped from the camp temporarily, the *commandant* got the sack. Many speculations concerning his probable successor were indulged in, and I think the general opinion of the camp was that the newcomer might be better, though he could not be worse. We soon discovered our mistake. His first appearance was not exactly promising. Two fellows while walking round the camp suddenly heard a stream of abuse violently directed at them, and looking up, they saw the *commandant* coming towards them through a gate in the wire, fairly bursting with rage. His unreasonable complaint was that he had not been saluted while entering his office outside the wire!

The offenders were at once packed off to cells for two or three days. The next day a few Britishers arrived from another camp, and while they were waiting outside to be admitted, a small and orderly crowd collected on the inside to see if they could recognise anyone, or exchange a few remarks. Being unable to walk much I watched the proceedings from the window of my room and was able to see everything that took place.

Without any warning the mad *commandant* rushed out of a building and up to the wire, where he screamed at the little gathering like a madman, making violent motions to show that they were to go back. It is perfectly legitimate to stand in a group as long as everyone behaves and no one touches the neutral zone wire. One must stand somewhere. In this case he had absolutely no right to order a move. The interpreter, who happened to be near, walked up and said that the *commandant* desired us to go away, whereupon the officers began to disperse, wishing to humour him. I was startled to see two soldiers come through the gate with fixed bayonets in a quick business-like way, to drive the fellows back faster, evidently by the *commandant's* express orders.

The younger of the two guards went straight up to an unoffending medical student, a Lieutenant Downes (S. Staffs.), who was then turning round, and pricked him in the stomach with his bayonet. To prevent the steady pressure making the slight wound worse, Downes seized the end of the rifle and, jerking the point out, swung it to the right, and then turning round walked quickly back. The sentry, after running past several other officers, overtook him and, to my horror, stuck the bayonet into his back. After continuing his walk for a few steps Downes collapsed and was at once carried into hospital, the next day being taken to Hanover. The wound was very serious, however; we received a message from the hospital a few days later stating that the bayonet had penetrated into one lung, but that he was getting on well and would probably soon recover.

The same sentry, in his eagerness to obey orders, tried to bayonet a Captain Woodhouse, but as his prey jumped back just in time, only succeeded in cutting the skin. By this time a large crowd had collected, which the sentries continued slowly forcing back, although they were then fifty yards from the wire. As the news spread the crowd became larger, but remained ominously quiet, the two Germans not seeming to realise the danger of their position. It is the worst feeling I know to watch a cowardly display of this sort and yet be able to do absolutely nothing. It only needed a spark to set everything in a blaze, which must have ended in the guard being turned out for machine-gun practice. Meanwhile, the news reached some Britishers who were half-way through a concert. By mutual consent it was at once broken up by the singing of the National Anthem. Everyone outside at once stood to attention and heartily joined in the last few bars.

It was the most impressive scene one could possibly imagine. I am sure that no one who had witnessed it would in after years, without feeling murder in his heart, watch a man belonging to the mongrel breed, which is not infrequently seen sitting down while everybody else is standing for the National Anthem, only being forced grudgingly to his feet by public opinion, even then not removing his hat unless it is knocked off. I am convinced that if Ramsay Macdonald and a few of his colleagues could have spent a week in a bad German prison camp they would be only too willing to instruct their misguided followers in singing "God Save the King," in the spirit and way in which it should be and was sung at Ströhen on July 15th, 1917. The situation was saved.

Our senior officer took advantage of the pause at the end while we were still under control, standing at attention, and told us to separate at once, as he would do everything that was possible. At this Israel departed every man to his own tent. The major asked for an immediate interview with the *commandant*, but the German captain who had entered replied that that was unfortunately impossible as that officer had gone out at lunch time and would not return till late. It was a most *"kolossal"* lie, but I do not think that the captain should be saddled with it, as he was, doubtless, acting under instructions. Most of those present, including myself, would have sworn on oath that we had seen the *commandant* a few minutes before and that he had caused all the trouble. But then what is one to do? Of course the usual complaints went (or rather were supposed to go) to higher authority (ambassadors and the like), but no satisfaction was obtained. It seems not unlikely that they all found their way into the office waste-paper basket by the most direct route.

Again, a few days later about a dozen fellows were watching a party of Germans, under a *Feldwebel* Pohlman, digging up an old tunnel which had fallen in near the wire. Everything was quiet and Pohlman was even talking naturally with one of our number, when I noticed him turn and speak a few words to the sergeant of the guard, who turned and entered the guardroom, evidently in a hurry. Knowing that this Pohlman, in spite of his oily manner and smug appearance, was a Hun in every sense of the word, I kept my weather eye open, warned the others and strolled off. A few seconds later four of the worst sentries in the place, having entered the camp unobserved, came running round the corner of a shed, their bayonets drawn back for thrusting, obviously having received orders that the next victim had to be finished off, the object, I suppose, being either to teach us a lesson or cause a mutiny.

Someone shouted a warning to three fellows who were standing talking to each other unconscious of their danger, but before they had time to realise their predicament the sentries were on them. The Huns singled out a Captain Wilson (R.F.C.), and before he could get away, surrounded him, while one villainous-looking little Hun lunged straight at him. By a quick movement Wilson avoided the thrust and succeeded in breaking away, the bayonet passing through his clothes. The guard continued to press everyone back into the centre of the camp, very serious trouble again only just being avoided.

Another incident of this sort happened a few days later, when to our surprise some strong sherry arrived at the canteen, and was soon bought up by the thirsty prisoners. I think there was another object in view, as well as a desire to make money. Towards evening some Englishmen were sitting near the wire, close to where the sentry who had assaulted Downes was stationed. One of the fellows, feeling a little cheerful, amused himself by alluding to the bravery of the act. At the worst this was only a case calling for a little solitary confinement. I suppose the sentry passed the word along to the guardroom, for soon three sentries passed through the camp, metaphorically whetting their bayonets, going towards the scene of the disturbance. Before reaching it they unslung their rifles and fixed their bayonets, doubled round the corner of the building, expecting to surprise the unfortunate Englander. But to their disgust they only found empty chairs and returned very dejected.

After this episode we had a dance in the dining-room, several fellows making up into the most charming girls, and did our best to forget our unpleasant surroundings. At ten o'clock, when we had gone to our barracks, according to the rules, Pohlman conducted an armed party of half a dozen Huns with fixed bayonets round the huts and every part of the camp, but failed to find the excuse he was longing for. Now what about the Cambrai officer's question, "Why do you call us Huns?" *Why, indeed?*

The German captain nearly always took roll call. Though fairly harmless, he was quite mad. He seldom brought an interpreter on parade and made long speeches and read orders to us, all in German, the great majority, of course, not understanding a single word! One day we heard the new *commandant* was coming on parade for the first time that evening, so therefore looked forward to some fun. When the time for the roll call arrived we were inspected as usual, and were standing waiting, when the little captain suddenly drew himself up to his full height, and screamed out: "*Augen Rechts—Augen Links—Gerade Aus.*" As we were standing in three sides of a square it was an order to make every one face the *commandant* with a martial air. The net result of this "Double Dutch" was that everyone broke into an amused smile, which increased almost to hysterics when we caught sight of the recipient of this honour. The *commandant* was a tall, doddery, antediluvian Prussian colonel, with long grey moustaches, the very image of the Monkey Brand advertisement, only perhaps not quite so good-looking. Why he did not fall over his trailing scabbard in every step remains a mystery to this day.

There was another curious little trick the captain sometimes indulged in. In the middle of delivering a tirade he would suddenly point to heaven with a dramatic gesture, as if to prove the truth of a recent statement by invoking the *Kaiser's* God. Perhaps someday he will learn that the popular spirit of Germany lives not above but very far below.

Soon after our arrival the prison was enlarged, as it always has to be when the camp becomes British. Fellows were often sent there for an offence about which they had never heard, without being able to say one word in self defence. In about two months I believe nearly half the camp had been in" clink." Until latterly it was forbidden to open windows at night, but being English we took the law into our own hands and continued opening the windows, refusing to be deprived of fresh air in the stifling heat. This naturally resulted in more prison, which at first relieved and then increased the monotony. Though it is hardly credible, our colonel had to carry out a sentence of three days "*stuben* arrest" for losing his poker! About this time an Australian was put into prison for a trivial offence which had been committed by someone else, and did not even receive his sentence for three whole weeks!

While in "jug" in this camp we were not allowed parcels, writing materials, books or smokes. We complained about this to a general who inspected the camp later; he expressed surprise at this state of affairs and had things partially rectified. For about two months all cigars and cigarettes received in parcels were stopped, the only reason given being that in some cases they had contained poison for destroying cattle. Not only were chances of destroying cattle exceedingly small, but we offered to smoke any cigarette they chose to give us from our parcels to prove the falsity of the charge.

By an agreement between the governments those serving terms of imprisonment for offences committed before the 4th of August, 1917, were released, a great number of the gaol-birds being sent to Ströhen. Residing in prison was a captain who made a hobby of being court-martialled. Under this new ruling he was taken out of cells for a few days, only to be put back to await trial for the trumped-up charge of having poison tablets on his person when recaptured after his last escape. I believe the only tablets he carried were either for purifying water, or Horlick's malted milk. Everyone recaptured when trying to escape in the late winter of 1916 or the following spring received a sentence of five months' imprisonment, a fortnight the original punishment, and the remainder as a supposed reprisal for the sentence given to escaping Germans in England.

The food given us was very bad indeed, though the list must have looked quite nice on paper. Apart from the eternal and loathsome gherkins, of which no mention was made, it asserted that we received fish twice a week! The Tuesday fish was of a dried variety, and had such a delicious smell when cooked that it was impossible to enter the dining-room when it was on the prowl! While that on Friday consisted of heaps of old mussels containing quantities of sand and young pebbles, known amongst ourselves as those —— barnacles, scraped from the ships at Kiel. The whole time I was there I never once had an opportunity of buying any fresh fruit, though it was summer time and we could have paid good prices. The only result of my bayoneting episode was that the sentry was congratulated, and I was warned for a court-martial!

When a staff captain arrived from Hanover to collect the evidence for the approaching trials, quite a cheery little crowd of accused officers were awaiting him. Several of them were to appear on two or three charges, and three R.F.C. officers were to be tried for dropping leaflets in the German lines. I believe it came to nothing in the end, as there was not enough evidence to convict them. Captain Scholtz and Lieutenant Wookey do not seem to have been so lucky. When my turn came, several German witnesses were produced who swore that after being struck on the foot with the butt, I had jumped forward to seize the rifle, asserting that the sentry had only acted in self-defence. (Such a truthful race!) When the captain was taking down my statement, we frequently got off the subject altogether. All of a sudden he would assert that the English had started the war and ask me the reason for their doing so.

Thoroughly roused, I would reply that it was nonsense and he must know it. Then ensued an amusing but fiery argument about the neutrality of Belgium, the use of native troops, and frightfulness in general. His plea was that poor little unoffending Germany was only standing up for herself against a set of blood-thirsty enemies who wished to crush her. Needless to say, I did not feel much like sympathising. When we finally got back to business, all particulars were taken as a matter of form, my slaughterer's name and address being taken down. Before my departure I managed to get a glimpse of it when the captain was out of the room. I do not suffer from loss of memory!

The all-absorbing problem of camp life is escaping. Up to this time half a dozen fellows had succeeded in getting away from the camp, but were afterwards recaptured. I will endeavour to give an outline of the several attempts and the difficulties to be overcome, which must of necessity be very curtailed, this book not being originally written for the benefit of the "Bosch." The most usual way is to cut the wire, but where sentries are numerous the undertaking is both difficult and dangerous. It is most natural to try stunts of the sort under cover of darkness. At this camp, however, the paraffin arc lamps were particularly brilliant, and when star-gazing on several occasions I have seen rats and mice scuttle across the white sand some distance away.

Though storms often raged during the day, the wind almost invariably blew itself out towards night, leaving a dead calm, broken only by the tramp of sentries or the distant rattling hum of a nightjar. It is a brave man who, having determined this mode of exit, leaves his hut when others are sleeping, and vanishes. Presently, if he gets safely across the intervening ground, the faint yet feverish snipping of wire-cutters is heard, each time being followed perhaps by a slight "ping" as the strained wire separates. The ensuing silence is almost heart-breaking, for in contrast something else may at any instant be increasing its tension, a sentry's trigger-finger.

One stormy night, when in hospital, I had reason to believe that an officer would make an attempt in that part of the camp at a given hour, so had an excellent chance of watching operations, which was not wasted. I went to the window and settled down for a long wait. Outside it was still raining, the sentries being in their boxes. A little before the time I caught sight of a dark figure which clambered out of the orderlies' hut and crawled into the neutral zone up to the outside wire, which he lay parallel to and commenced to cut. To my surprise, another figure joined him from the hut and lay there waiting; this was an orderly who had decided to join at the last instant. In about one and a half minutes a large enough gap had been cut, and the adventurers crawled through it, and were preparing to make a dash into the darkness when a sentry spotted them and stepped out of his box.

Having burned their boats, off they went. The sentry ran a few steps, then, stopping abruptly, raised his rifle and fired. It was an anxious moment for the onlookers; the fugitives already knew the result, while, as yet, we did not. However, to our relief, the ghost-like figures continued their flight until they were swallowed up in the darkness, and the reflection of the artificial light on their wet rain-coats became too weak to give away their position.

In their anxiety to leave the camp behind they tended to separate, but both fell headlong into a deep ditch, where they met again. In their first dash one of them dropped most of the provisions, which the Germans discovered and brought back to the camp in triumph. Six days afterwards they were recaptured, thirty kilometres from the border. Two officers cut the wire in broad daylight, when the nearest sentry was busy opening a gate admitting some orderlies. They left the camp by way of a ditch without being seen, crawling as they had never crawled before, their heads showing above the level of the fields, like two wobbling cabbages going for a hurried evening stroll. Their success was short-lived, for, only an hour afterwards, they were spotted and chased by some farmers, being finally brought to a stop by a man with a shot-gun. Another couple left the camp by the following ingenious method.

A captain, who spoke German like a native, dressed up in the clothes of a Hun private (somehow acquired). Some of the essential things were missing, and had been manufactured in secret, such as a cap and a painted wooden bayonet, with a lovely coloured tassel. When everything was ready, about ten o'clock one morning, a perfectly good German private marched an R.F.C. lieutenant, disguised as an orderly, who carried two buckets (containing their kit), up to a gate in the wire, which he rattled to signify that it must be unlocked immediately. The sentry came along, unlocked the gate, and let him out. They proceeded to the road, which they followed for a short distance.

That afternoon, while crossing a wild bit of country, they had the misfortune to be recaptured by a shooting party, being first completely surrounded by the beaters. Two other officers got out separately in an ingenious way, the first being recaptured crossing a bridge over the Ems, quite near Holland; the second lost direction, and was retaken four days after, having got thoroughly lost. One unlucky person was collared just outside the wire, dressed as an orderly, and was taken straight to prison to enjoy a period of perfect rest!

I worked in several tunnels at different times, fitted with air pumps and perhaps even electric light—who knows? Digging oneself out is, at the best of times, a slow and difficult proposition, which is almost invariably discovered sooner or later. The humorous side of tunnelling is so pronounced that, could "Bairnsfather" view one such episode, our bookstalls would shortly be surrounded by eager crowds, clamouring for the first edition of *Fragments from Germany*, depicting mud-bespattered "Old Bills" crawling for their very lives down narrow tunnels, closely pursued by the wily Hun!

About this time I made my second attempt to escape, and succeeded in getting outside the wire for the time being, early one afternoon during bathing hours, only to discover that my proposed hiding-place was occupied by Germans. After sitting solemnly beside my kit for an hour, expecting discovery every second, I was lucky enough to return, unmolested, with a party of bathers. During this period of anxious waiting I was surprised to find that the thought of losing my carefully prepared outfit was considerably more distressing than the actual prospect of imprisonment.

CHAPTER 9

"An Outlaw Once Again"

When a sufficient number of officers had collected for baths at a little gate, a sentry allowed them to pass through it and along a short, wired path, or bird-cage (as we called it), and thence into the bathroom. This room was situated about ten yards outside the wire, in the middle of a wooden barrack, running parallel to, and about fifteen yards away from, the wire. It is subdivided to form a dressing-room and a place for the shower baths, every exit being strongly barred, and a sentry stationed at the door. After a minute inspection of every nook and cranny, I found that it was just possible, by standing upright, to squeeze into an alcove, about eleven inches deep and a foot wide, in an angle formed by a wall and the brickwork of a chimney which projected into the room.

Though in full view of the door, it was partially hidden behind an empty stove. I reasoned that, should a well-made dummy wall obscure the aperture, it would take a very observant sentry to detect anything amiss. As a last resource, even should it be noticed, it might pass as something to do with the heating of the adjacent room. After weighing up the chances of success for several days, I decided that it was worth trying. When the measurements had been taken, behind the Bosch's back, I set to work to manufacture the false wall.

Most of my friends ridiculed the idea, calling my pet wall a doll's house and other insulting names, and bestowing on me much superfluous sympathy and pity. They argued that it had not been done before, and was, therefore, impossible, doing their level best to stop me embarking on such a mad enterprise. At first they almost succeeded in their object, but, knowing that most ordinary people remain in a camp indefinitely, working on more orthodox lines, I determined that I would put it to the test, if only to prove them wrong, or land myself in prison. One infantry officer, who had previously been through a course of camouflage, gave me his moral support, which counted for a good deal.

The wall was made of cardboard sewn tightly on to a light wooden frame, the whole being made in three sections, which, when fitted together, reached the height of about eight feet six inches. The top section was fitted with a leather hinge, which allowed the upper half of it to slope back at an angle of forty-five degrees, so that the hiding-place should not appear to be hollow. When at last the doll's house was finished, it defied all efforts to whiten it, and seemed to have a rooted objection to being made to resemble the dirty whitewash of the bath-room. I tried melting old whitewash (scraped off the walls) with gum and hot water, but it either fell off when dry or showed the wet cardboard plainly through. Chloride of lime proved equally useless. Only a little white paint was procurable, but this was altogether too smooth and shiny.

One day, when the three sections were drying outside on the sand, a German *feldwebel* (sergeant-major—commonly known as a "field-wobble") came along, and inquired if I was making a model aeroplane. When I replied that his surmise was correct, he asked me, with a slow smile, if I intended flying away when the machine was completed. The wicked old creature departed, highly amused at my answer, "Yes, I hope so." Certainly many a true word is spoken in jest!

After a week's experimenting with useless colouring mixtures, I was almost in despair, when the desired effect was produced by coating the cardboard with a thick cornflour paste, finally toning it down with a mixture of cobwebs and mud.

Though on three separate occasions I had everything ready for the final test, it was not before August 16th that conditions were at last favourable enough to risk my welfare for the next few weeks. A little before five o'clock I entered the bathroom, accompanied by several assistants. Our journey thither was rather amusing, though the slightest accident would have meant much "*stuben* arrest." It is not easy to walk naturally when carrying a young wall out of sight under one's coat, which is doing its best to give the show away by shedding bits of plaster which fall to the ground and leave a trail, reminding one strongly of a paper chase.

However, the sentries noticed nothing unusual. As soon as the Hun's back was turned I slipped the sections together and squeezed into the alcove, into which I was securely fastened by a friend, who whispered that everything looked O.K., and asked me to be sure and write to him when I got to England. Whether this was meant or not I do not know, but at any rate it was just the encouragement I needed. It was an anxious moment when everybody left the room with a final "Good luck," and I heard the sentry approaching to make sure that nobody had been left behind.

Previously I had determined not to watch the Hun, as my gaze might render him more liable to look in my direction. Now, under the stress of circumstances, this seemed a physical impossibility, and all good resolutions went to the winds. I glued one eye to the spy-hole and saw a German standing only a few feet away, with his back to me, puffing solemnly at a long pipe, a rifle slung over his shoulder. Almost immediately, as if in answer to my concentrated gaze, he turned and looked straight in my direction. I promptly shrivelled up to nothing, and developed acute suspended animation. I simply dared not breath, and felt as if my thoughts were becoming audible. My relief was indescribable when he turned away, and left in an ordinary manner. Though one crisis was over, the strain had been such that it took me several minutes to "defossilise" and grasp the fact that, somewhere in the dim distance, the chances of success were increasing.

A few minutes later a N.C.O. came in, and searched about for soap. As he was pocketing some small bits left behind, my wall threatened to fall outwards, but I managed to hold it steady until he went away. A five-and-a-half hour wait lay in front of me, and, my prison being dark, stifling and hot, the time passed intolerably slowly. After waiting patiently for what I judged to be anything from half to three-quarters of an hour, I would glance at my watch, only to discover that, in reality, four or five minutes had passed. My primary success was evidently well known inside the camp, for most of the fellows taking their evening stroll cast anxious veiled glances in my direction, from the wrong side of the wire.

It was with both pleasure and anxiety that I watched the darkness slowly closing in, though I felt inclined to disbelieve that "*Time and tide wait for no man.*" Half-past ten did eventually arrive, and with it the now unwelcome time for action. Slowly, and with infinite caution, I stepped out into the room, and replaced the wall to give someone else a chance later on. Most of my kit was in the stove, and, as there were no fire-irons about, considerable noise was made lifting the iron top and extracting the contents with my fingers. Everything was now squashed into a sort of pack, and I approached the window on tiptoe.

Within the camp all was quiet, but there, just outside, passing and re-passing on his beat, often not ten yards away, was a particularly young and active German sentry, stepping quietly, with an elastic tread. He held his rifle in his hands, and gazed intently into the camp, as if expecting some shooting practice. When he reached the end of his short beat, I opened the door with many misgivings, and crept along a passage to the back of the hut. Entering the empty wash-room, I saw that my information had been correct, the windows were not barred. In an adjoining room several Huns were settling down for the night, their light showing under the door.

I had almost reached the nearest window when, with a most appalling crash, I overturned an empty bucket in the dark. Listening an instant, I heard surprised voices and waited for no further developments, but, coat, pack and all, jumped through the half-open window and fell into a ditch below. Struggling up and tripping over another wire, I landed in another ditch. After leaving this my way lay beyond the shadow of the hut across a cultivated patch of moor, planted with potatoes, which was illuminated by the arc lamps. I covered this in record time, everything rattling and seeming to make a most deafening noise, as though all the devils in Hell were after me with red-hot pitchforks, expecting to hear a bullet whistle by every moment. However, nothing happened, and when several hundred yards away, I halted for about ten minutes to listen for the bugle sounding the alarm. It would have been some satisfaction to know that the camp was buzzing like a beehive, and all on my account! But, owing to the clever way in which my roommates worked it, my absence was not noticed, and so this pleasure was denied me.

I shouldered my heavy pack and started out over the heather in the direction indicated by the stars. The greatest obstacles were the peat bogs, into which I often sank knee-deep, and had to crawl out. After about two hours rough walking, I was lying among the heather resting, when I was startled by a slight noise like the rattle of a chain. Looking up quickly as the moon came out from behind a cloud, I saw a dark shape, which seemed to move considerably closer and a little to the left, as I watched. A general survey of my position was not reassuring, for, in the light, I could distinctly see half-a-dozen more dark forms situated on my front and sides at regular intervals, mostly in a crouching position.

Instantly I thought that somehow I had been traced by dogs, and that these were sentries. Knowing the gentle way in which the inmates of this camp were treated, I must confess that I was very scared. I had not even a stick; besides, one could wish for a more congenial meeting-place to accost gentlemen of this sort than a lonely moor at midnight. Behind me was a long cutting, filled with dark water, from which peat had been taken; into this I cautiously slid up to my shoulders, and waited developments. Nothing happened, and, as I became colder and colder, I began to think that, after all, I had been mistaken. Was it possible that they were only heaps of peat? At last I summoned up enough courage to crawl out and approach one of the mysterious forms. Still nothing happened, and my confidence increased considerably. I had only gone a few yards when I saw that it was actually only a heap of peat with a large piece lying near the top which protruded sideways, this having formed the supposed sentry's head. Even then I did not feel quite convinced until I administered a hard kick and there was no retaliation.

During the night I passed several villages, and once found myself among a lot of small apple trees, which I shook violently. Down tumbled some unripe fruit. It did not take long to fill my pockets and clear off at full speed. Towards morning I lost sight of the camp lights, and, entering a small fir plantation, arranged a good hiding-place and soon fell asleep. In less than an hour I awoke in a soaking condition, and sat up with a start, the only result being that the movement shook the fir branches over my head, and a shower-bath ensued. The next day I enjoyed five thunderstorms! No sooner had one passed over than another came up. My homemade tent, a large sheet of green oil-silk, smuggled from home, kept off a good deal of the rain, but, nevertheless, I had a good opportunity of studying the condition of a half-drowned rat. In spite of the wet and the presence of some large wood-ants, I rather enjoyed the sour apples, the first I had tasted that summer. Once during the afternoon a red squirrel came jumping over the fir needles, and looked up impudently into my face. The sight of so much ugliness almost overcame him, but he managed to scamper off at a good speed. I tried hard to attract this, my only friend, by pretending to be Hiawatha, and calling him an "*Adjidaumo*," but this only hurried his retreat.

My food consisted mostly of chocolate and biscuits, though, for the first three days, I did not feel at all hungry. Water was very scarce, but I received more than my share a few days later. The third night, leaving the moon behind, I climbed over a barbed wire fence, and found myself among a lot of large and bony black-and-white Holstein cattle. Murmuring soft German words of endearment, I approached the nearest cow in the hope of obtaining some milk. However, these good creatures, thinking it a most unusual milking hour, were not having any, and showed their disapproval of my conduct by careering madly round the field, making a fiendish noise, which caused the author of the disturbance to take to his heels for fear of discovery. A little later I changed my tactics.

After stealing several luscious apples, I presented them to another walking milk-tank. The creature had a softer heart, and succumbed to the temptation. Everything went according to plan, for, while she munched the apple contentedly, I proceeded to fill a large tin mug several times over. I tramped for ten nights, and only missed my milk three times. Another night, passing in front of a farm-house, I came upon a full milk-can standing by a gate; the contents not only filled my water bottle, but even satisfied me.

One morning, after an unusually long march, I flopped down and went to sleep in an overgrown ditch, surrounded by gorse and broom. The sun was just rising when I awoke with the idea that I was lying on a bed of pins. The idea grew to a firm conviction when an involuntary movement of mine considerably increased my discomfort. As I lay trying to solve the problem in a semi-conscious condition, the solution ran across my face; it seemed to have a great many legs. As my fingers closed round it I received another violent pin-prick, but held on manfully and, with an effort, forced myself to look at my prey. It was a gigantic angry wood-ant, which hung on to my finger for all it was worth. Considering the two things which terrify me most are ants and centipedes, perhaps the reader will understand my perturbed state of mind when I found myself lying beside a large ants' nest, being slowly devoured by its inhabitants, like a fat green caterpillar.

As if propelled by a rocket I sprang up, and ran up and down the short ditch at full speed. When fatigue had brought me to a stop I was delighted to find that they had mostly been shaken off out of my clothes. It was impossible to find a resting place free from ants, the whole place was infested with them. In my efforts to avoid them I climbed to the top of a thick pine tree, but even there my little friends were parading along the branches. The day proved to be so hot and thundery that, before twelve o'clock, the milk in my bottle turned solid and had to be eaten like junket. It was with great satisfaction that I watched the darkness setting in, for, under its protection, I was enabled to leave the unholy spot and continue my nightly travels.

One of the things which had troubled me considerably when planning my escape was how to reset my watch should it go wrong. As it was, the village clocks kept me well informed by striking the hour with much vigour. The next day, as I lay hidden at the edge of a very young plantation, a party of labourers with scythes assembled not far away. After leaving their coats and, presumably, their provisions behind, they proceeded to cut the grass along the edge of the plantation and in a neighbouring field. As I lay "doggo" I formulated many plans for stealing their food to replenish my store, but finally decided that the risk was too great. Only once did I think that I had been discovered, for, as I was passing my time in a wood by carving a souvenir stick, something burst close beside me, making quite a commotion and breaking many twigs. Just before the branches closed I caught sight of a fluffy white tail. After all it was only a frightened deer.

Late on the sixth night I was walking fast along the side of a road which led through a forest when, stopping an instant to listen, I heard a low voice shout about forty yards in front. Then someone approached with a previously concealed lantern. Instantly I jumped over the ditch, hoping to get away under the trees unnoticed. Unfortunately, I landed on some dry twigs, which crackled at every step and betrayed my presence. Remembering the deer incident, I emitted a loud, coughing bark, such as those animals make, and crashed through the undergrowth, making as much noise as possible. To my relief I saw that the man with the lantern turned back to his post to rejoin his companion—presumably the ruse succeeded. It was just as well I was not caught here, for now I have reason to believe that I was close to an important aerodrome, and that this was a guard—possibly against espionage.

The distance covered was, roughly, a hundred and sixty miles, and, during the whole period, only once did I recognise the name of a small town on a milestone, which told me I was going in the right direction. The fact of having no one to talk to for so many days, combined with the uncertainty of it all, had the most depressing influence. While waiting for the long days to pass, killing countless mosquitoes, I frequently wondered if the stars could be purposely leading me in the wrong direction, or if peace had been declared, and I was on an unnecessarily tiring walking tour.

As I was approaching a busy railway, I frequently heard thuds and crashes, or, if the wind was steady, a faint roar, which, I afterwards found, was caused by the continued traffic and shunting of trucks. This troubled me quite a lot, for it sounded exactly like an intermittent bombardment, and not infrequently increased in volume, until I am convinced an old soldier would have sworn it was a distant barrage. I pictured my arrival at the frontier only to learn that Holland had decided to be in the fashion, and was therefore running a little war on her own, on the popular Bolshevik excuse of upholding the cause of democracy. The only thing left for me to do would have been to have turned about and, after many trials and hardships, succeed in getting into Switzerland, where Fate, with a smile on her face, would probably have arranged to have me shot by accident while on my way through Zurich, during the subsequent riots.

Our "*moutons*" in the meantime, have been straying badly; it is, therefore, our duty to leave dreams to take care of themselves, and return to the subject without more ado. When I had been on the loose for a week the country became very flat and sodden—water was everywhere. Most of the roads were banked up to guard against flood, while all ditches were transformed into small canals. Trees became scarcer and, consequently, the daily problem of finding effectual cover increased in difficulty. Nearly all the seventh night I followed a tow-path at the side of an important canal, which led in a northerly direction. Innumerable movable bridges, traversing the lesser waterways which flowed into the big canal, had to be crossed.

This procedure was more alarming than one might suppose, as the frail bridges shook at the slightest touch, and also advertised my crossing to the inmates of the usual adjoining lodge by magnifying every little sound. Most of the way, moored at the water's edge, were barges laden with peat, containing all sorts of dogs; in fact, in several instances they seemed to be veritable floating dogs' homes. These creatures barked as if paid to, and were usually sympathetically answered by dogs some distance in advance, thus inadvertently proclaiming the news of my arrival. Once two men came out of a cottage twenty yards ahead, and, stopping in the path, turned round and watched me approaching. That time I really thought the game was up.

It was absolutely essential to maintain a bold exterior, despite the fact that my breathing apparatus almost ceased to work. Slouching quickly along, I whistled a bar or two of "*Püppchen.*" Curiously enough my presence at that time of night created no suspicion, for I passed them without being spoken to. Before taking a road leading to the west, I sat down and dissolved my last Oxo cube in a mug of cold, greenish canal water. The meal is prepared as follows: First suck your middle finger until it tastes clean, then stir the Oxo until it is dissolved (this usually takes about half an hour). Before drinking the concoction it is necessary to remove any dead fishes that may be floating on the surface, and also make certain that none of the Oxo is wasted by remaining underneath the finger nails.

At intervals I was very gratified to see that the sky, to the north and north-east, was illuminated by distant searchlights. As several naval bases lay in that direction, it is reasonable to suppose that the Huns were expecting a visit from our airmen. After following the road for over an hour, I procured some excellent apples at a wayside farmhouse, and beat a hasty retreat. As time wore on and the milk carts began rumbling on their rounds, I quickened my pace and commenced a desperate search for cover. Leaving the road, I headed across the fields, and after jumping, or falling into, several flooded ditches, came to an overgrown marsh. A few yards from *terra firma* was a large sallow bush, growing on a tiny island. After getting thoroughly wet, I succeeded in crawling on to this and screening my headquarters from prying eyes with green rushes.

As it became lighter, I heard occasional voices and peculiar creakings, the cause of which I could not interpret, and might well render my position unsafe. The anxiety was increased when a large, dark shadow loomed out of the fog and threatened to completely swallow my little island. All at once the curling white mist drifted away, and everything was explained in an instant. The terrifying shadow resolved itself into the great red-brown sail of a passing barge. I was lying close beside the tow-path of a canal. Just as the sun had risen over the trees and the mists were beginning to disperse and float upwards, another noise attracted my attention, which developed into a deep throbbing roar. Looking up, I saw three large" Zepps," flying low, and rolling slightly in the stiff morning breeze, returning to their lair after a strenuous night out. As they passed over the school-children in a neighbouring village cheered excitedly.

Except for the usual mosquito bites and inability to sleep, the day passed uneventfully. When darkness fell and all was quiet again, I once more saddled up and started out, this time earnestly hoping, yet fearing, to reach the river Ems, which had to be swum whatever happened. About midnight I came to something concrete at last—a long-expected railway. After a short reconnaissance, I crossed this, and made my way over the fields towards the all-important river, which flowed parallel to the frontier and about twenty kilos away from it. Every few yards I came to a dyke, which always had to be passed through if the direction was to be kept. It was an odious experience, for, no sooner did I emerge dripping from one than it was time to enter the next.

About three o'clock, after milking several cows and swimming a few small canals, I passed through some open flood-gates, built in a grass ridge made to keep the water from encroaching on the low-lying farms, and came upon a most disheartening sight. Beyond several hundred yards of dangerous marsh flowed the river, looking very white in the deceptive light of early morning. The wavelets formed by the steady wind and the current were making a faint, but disconcerting, noise. Though it was only just possible to discern the opposite bank, there seemed to be a similar line of marshy ground between it and the water's edge. I determined to see if it was possible to get through the marsh with any degree of safety, but gave up the idea when some of the old decayed reeds on which I was standing suddenly gave way and let me through into the water up to my waist.

No matter how good a swimmer, a reedy swamp is more than one can contend with, therefore I gave up the idea. Crawling out and walking a little way along the bank, something loomed up in front of me out of the darkness, which turned out to be a long iron bridge. Looking cautiously along it, I saw a couple of dim lights burning near the other side. What an easy way over; how I should have loved to stroll across; but it could not be, for a German guard was waiting there to receive me with open arms. Reluctantly I turned away and struck inland, intending to travel parallel to the river for some distance and then try my luck at another place. Shortly afterwards, when tramping along on the grass at the side of a road in search of a hiding-place, I heard footsteps approaching.

At either side of the road grew a row of young trees, but, unfortunately, the trunks were not large enough to hide behind. The conditions were such as to render discovery inevitable should a hasty retirement be effected. For several precious seconds I stood paralysed with indecision, seeing my danger, yet unable to avoid it; meanwhile it seemed that cruel fate was carelessly deciding my destiny, weighing freedom against captivity in a balance, which my indecision was slowly causing to turn against me. For a brief period my brain refused to work, except vaguely to bring to my notice a few lines from *Eldorado*, which affirm that there exists a loophole of escape in every difficult situation. This seemed to affect my present critical position, though it in no wise suggested a course of action.

As I looked at the dyke which ran along at the side of the raised road, calculating that the noise made by a passage through it would only lead to detection, I clearly remembered an incident in *Lorna Doone*, in which John Ridd, when a boy, had completely avoided discovery by his enemy (Carver Doone) by submerging himself in a stream and breathing through a straw. Without waiting to remove the pack, I followed his example by throwing myself on my face and crawling backwards on to the tangled reeds, which parted with a squelch and let me through into the stagnant water. The dyke proved to be deeper than I expected. My feet barely touched the bottom, so that I was literally clutching a straw to keep myself up.

As the footsteps passed I kept my face and head under the surface, and trusted to Providence. When all the sounds died away, it took me some time struggling with mud, weeds and water, before I could extricate myself from that confounded ditch. I do not make a good water-rat; I would therefore suggest to the German authorities that they should train water spaniels, and not police dogs, for pursuit of prisoners in the future.

I had only been walking for a little while when the distant rumble of a milk-cart reminded me that it was past time to hibernate. Then began the usual desperate search for cover. It became lighter and lighter, and, just as the mist was about to rise, I saw the faint outline of a clump of trees several hundred yards away. Plunging through more dykes I arrived at the trees, only to find that they were growing in a small garden and orchard which surrounded a large farmhouse. As no one appeared to be stirring, and the discovery of an immediate hiding-place was essential, I commenced explorations. The privet hedge surrounding this oasis proved to be very thin and there were no convenient little bushes. I had just borrowed a good supply of apples from mine host, and had almost decided to seek shelter in an outhouse as a last resource, when I came upon a fair-sized heap of sticks, over which a hop plant sprawled, forming a straggly green covering.

There being no better place, I decided that the hop would have to serve as my headquarters for that day. I was just moving some of the sticks when something caused me to remember the lateness of the hour. From a pigsty a few yards away came expectant squeals. The occupants doubtless imagined that I was arriving with their breakfast. As I was getting ready to crawl into the sticks, I caught sight of a little patch of washing close by, lying spread on the grass at the corner of a small green lawn. When the good lady came for her washing she would, in all probability, discover me, which would never do, as it would lead to all kinds of little unpleasantnesses.

In a very short space of time I had moved the white handkerchiefs and collars to another corner of the lawn, not far away, and returned to the heap. I was beginning to tunnel into the sticks, when I heard a man's voice, followed by the clatter of milk cans. Diving into the small hole already made, I wriggled for all I was worth towards the centre, dragging the pack after me. It sounds quite simple; all you have to do is to wriggle; but, in reality, it is surprisingly difficult. When I tried to force an entrance every dead bough in the heap seemed to break with an ear-splitting crash, while all the smaller twigs crackled in chorus. The most peaceable sticks developed sharp spikes, which stuck into me. Even when I had removed a particularly objectionable one barring the way, another would shoot out and grasp my pack, causing an additional delay.

Eventually, in a scratched and weary condition, I got under the centre of the heap, where I lay feeling none too secure. Although I was forced to keep still for fear of attracting attention, I managed to nibble the stolen apples and take stock of my surroundings. The light shone through the pale green hop leaves, revealing many hairy caterpillars, incessantly gorging. Inside the heap lived innumerable spiders and other horrors. These believed in making their presence felt when I did not deign to notice them. It was a very uncomfortable procedure, drying slowly in a cold wind. Once, when the leaves blew on one side, I caught a glimpse of a pear tree swaying overhead, and a dark, forbidding sky in the background.

That day I enjoyed two heavy thunderstorms. At first the leaves kept off most of the rain, but it soon battered down with such violence that the former became limp and hung down, leaving me almost exposed. Everything became saturated. A steady stream of water poured off the sticks and ran down my neck, while the insects eagerly sought shelter in my clothing. When the first storm was over, and I lay shivering in the bright interval, two children came out of the house and played about in the garden, running several times round and round my heap. It was such a strain lying absolutely still that I almost welcomed the second thunderstorm, though it completely soaked everything that the first one had overlooked.

Never in my life have I passed such an uncomfortable day. But, in the end, discomfort is preferable to actual danger in an adventure of this sort. At least so I thought in those days. As it is beyond me to convey to the reader any adequate idea of the unwillingness of the minutes to resolve themselves into hours, I will not attempt the impossible. Towards evening someone fired a shot-gun just beyond the privet hedge. Naturally the explosion caused me to jump, but that was nothing to the fright I experienced when it struck me that it might be a small boy out rat shooting, as vermin always run to a conveniently close heap of sticks for shelter. However, the person did not come my way, and in any case it is probable he was only after wild duck, which frequent most of the dykes. At last, when I could stand it no longer, I scrambled out into the dusk, guiltily ignoring the fact that I was running an unnecessary risk by starting on the war-path an hour too soon.

CHAPTER 10

The Ems

There was no one about, so, after enjoying a good stretch, I pushed through the privet, jumped a narrow dyke, and started out over the low-lying fields towards the high grassy barrier which advertised the approach to the dreaded river. It was almost dark when I came to another portion of the winding, snake-like barrier, which curved out as if to meet me. Approaching it, I found that a thick and apparently endless prickly May hedge grew along the base. Getting through it proved to be such a painful proceeding that it seems probable that as soon as the hedge saw an Englishman coming towards it, it sharpened its claws and resolved to defend the way to the frontier to the last thorn. Of course I may be wrong in my surmise, but I well remember that, when I began extracting thorns afterwards, it was like plucking a pin-cushion. Crawling on hands and knees up the slippery grassy slope, I soon arrived at the top and, scrambling to my feet, looked eagerly towards the unknown West.

The grassy barrier rose to an even height of about thirty feet above the low-lying country. On one side, the nearer dykes dividing the fields showed up a dull white in the semi-darkness; while on the other, beyond a narrow fringe of swaying reed-grass, ran the broad dark river. Although a steady wind was blowing, it was not quite as strong as on the previous night, the noise of the ripples breaking on the shore not being so pronounced. As I had not been dry for several days, the prospect of a prolonged bathe was not at all alluring. The longer I looked towards the opposite bank the more distant it appeared to be, and the greater became the width and volume of the river, until it seemed to be quite impassable. Hesitation meant failure, so, running down to the water's edge, I began to undress quickly. All at once it struck me that it would be foolish to wrap all my earthly belongings in one bundle, for, should it come to grief on the way over, I should have a decidedly cool time of it after my arrival at the other bank of the river.

Besides, it would be most undignified to be compelled to walk up to a German sentry and address him thus: "Please, sir, I am suffering from loss of memory and seem to have mislaid my clothes; would you be good enough to supply me with a few, as fig trees do not abound in these parts?"

Therefore, spreading my sodden waterproof on the ground, I deposited in it my tunic, shoes and now half-empty pack. Stuffing all the vacant space tightly with grass, I secured the corners by binding them together with my braces and bits of torn handkerchief. To complete the operation, I fastened my souvenir walking-stick (which, though large and clumsy, was exceedingly precious) to the bottom of the bundle in order to improve its floating capacities. Passing through the thin edging of reed-grass, I stepped into the shallow water and felt my feet sink into the deep mud, which gurgled hungrily and sent little lines of bubbles up to the surface. In a few strides I was out of my depth and amid the swirling eddies, which sought to drag me off downstream.

Fortunately the water was warm and the bundle floated well. Considering the fact that I had already been tramping for eight days on short rations, it is not surprising that I found swimming against a steady wind to be very tiring. I kept the bundle well ahead by giving it a good push every few strokes, when I overtook it. After swimming for several minutes, I unconsciously changed my direction a little, at the same time giving the bundle another push ahead. At this part the river curved slightly, and the result was that the wind caught my worldly belongings and whirled them off downstream. Signalling to the engine-room for full speed ahead, I dashed off in pursuit, soon overtaking the runaway bundle.

By this time, being very out of breath, I hung on to it, and was delighted to find that it would practically support me. I had been swimming for some little time and it seemed probable that my objective would not be far away, so, looking up at the stars and noting where the west lay, I raised myself in the water and looked for the opposite bank. Curiously enough, it seemed almost as far distant as it had been at first. Instinctively I looked back, and there, only a little way behind me, was the shore I had just left. I must admit that the sight was not encouraging. Well—hanging on to a waterlogged bundle and swallowing tadpoles would not help matters, so I settled down to business, swimming steadily on my side, but often changing the stroke, and heading a little upstream to counteract the force of the current.

Ever so gradually the water became calmer and the shore more clearly defined, until I could see a fringe of weeds similar to the one I had left. Vaguely I wondered if it would be really worth the extra effort required to actually reach it. It seemed so easy to give up. Just as I felt my remaining strength slipping away at each stroke I touched some soft warm mud. Mud as a rule does not have a stimulating effect on one, but then the very touch of it put new life into me. Dragging my bundle, I made a final effort to get ashore, but fell in the shallow water, where I lay utterly exhausted, hardly conscious of my surroundings, my head sinking gradually lower and lower. It must have been the objectionable taste of the muddy water which brought me to my senses sufficiently to enable me to leave the river for a more congenial resting place, namely, some grass at the edge of a field. When at last I got up, feeling very cold, and untied the bundle I found that everything was absolutely soaking. Assuredly there are many more enjoyable pastimes than putting on wet clothes in a cold wind in the dark.

When everything was ready for the night's tramp, I discovered that my cap was missing, and after a short fruitless search, decided to leave it behind. Tired, shivering, and hatless, I started off into the West, reckoning that now the frontier could not be much more than a night's march away. No sooner had I crossed the little stubble field than I came to a ridge, beyond which the ground dropped several feet in a steep slope. As I moved down this incline towards what appeared to be a hedge, the ground became quite wet. Suspiciously I looked ahead into the darkness towards what seemed to be only an expanse of lower ground. Near the hedge the water rose over my ankles, but I forged on, determined to know the worst. I was not long in suspense, for the hedge in front rustled (a thing that well-trained hedges do not do), and I knew that it was another long line of high reed-grass.

Fearfully I parted this with my hands, and there, in front, lay a rippling sheet of water, fully as wide as the river I had just crossed. With a thump my heart went down into my boots, and the little devil of despair whispered that I must be near the mouth of the river, on an island, a prisoner of my own making. (In truth, this was very nearly the case, for, as I feared, I was very far north, this accounting for the volume and width of the river.) This stretch of water was totally unexpected. Had I been fresh and known my whereabouts, it would have formed a formidable enough obstacle; as it was, I had already done more than my share of bathing for that night, and knew that I was in a totally unfit condition to attempt another long-distance swim.

Obviously the first thing to be done was to make certain that I was indeed on an island, so I proceeded to take stock of my surroundings. I noticed that, except for the rough patches on the water which caught the wind, the surface was comparatively smooth, and there was no sign of a current. Walking a few yards to the right, I saw that the line of the old river and this strip of unknown water converged, leaving little hope in that direction. I therefore turned about, and started off to my left front. Evidence that the cereal crop had been carted quite recently was plentiful, for there was short, fresh stubble, cart tracks, and the impression of horses' hoofs. This pointed to the encouraging fact that I was not on an island, horses and carts not usually being transported by barge or aeroplane.

I had not followed the tracks for more than fifty yards when they turned straight towards the water. The next minute I barely stifled a yell of delight, for there, staring me in the face, was a sort of pontoon bridge, stretching away into the darkness. On closer inspection, I found it to be composed of bundles of brushwood which were held together in some mysterious manner, and appeared to lie on the water. The surface of the bridge was in very bad repair and, as some of the top bundles of sticks were missing or pointing upwards at an angle, progress was very slow; but, sometimes walking, sometimes crawling, I got along at quite a good pace. Once it seemed that I should have to swim a short distance, but I found it to be unnecessary, as only the top layer of the bundles was missing.

Nearing the other side, I made out a factory building of some sort, with a high chimney, a little way from the end of the bridge, and heard the occasional bark of a watch-dog. Try as I would, I could not move an inch without causing a number of sticks to crackle loudly—it was almost as bad as crawling under the heap of sticks the morning before. Fortunately the wind must have drowned any noise made, or carried the sound away, for, though the dog continued to bark intermittently, it cannot have been aware of my presence.

Skirting the factory, I went across country, avoiding roads and houses like poison. The land was very low and flat and the dykes very numerous, sometimes whole fields being practically inundated. The only things that tended to relieve the monotony were the solitary gaunt willow trees, most of them mere shells of their former selves, which stood out from the misty darkness, black and threatening, like grim sentinels.

Everywhere was water, water, water. Every few seconds I was up to my waist in it. Often I tried to jump a narrow dyke and misjudged the distance, or got a bad "take off," owing to the softness of the ground; this usually resulted in my falling with a splash into the middle. I think the most aggravating thing of all was to make a really good jump and land on the other side, just beyond the water-line, on all fours, only to find that I had not enough impetus to remain there, as the ground was sloping. Sometimes I was able to save myself by jabbing my stick into the ground, though, more often than not, this was impracticable, and my hands could find nothing firmer to catch hold of than a few tufts of grass, which almost invariably gave way, causing me to do a graceful but involuntary backward dive into the dyke.

As constant exercise of this sort is very tiring and the weight of water contained in one's clothes greatly hinders freedom of action, my progress was necessarily rather slower than usual. A little after midnight the ground became harder, and I soon found myself once more on a moor, wandering along a narrow sandy track, among deep heather and broom bushes. Just as I was getting a little drier and it seemed as if the watery nightmare was over, I ran into a series of peat bogs, many of them more dangerous than those I had encountered my first night out.

I found the best way to cross a narrow strip of marsh was to make a rush to the firm ground, as these tactics did not allow enough time for my feet to sink in very far. Once the little track I was cautiously following ended abruptly at the edge of a particularly watery-looking bog, which not only barred my way in front, but also curved round on both flanks. In order to avoid this *cul-de-sac* it would have been necessary to make a wide detour, the accomplishment of which would have involved the wasting of much valuable time. Selecting a point where this strip of marshy ground appeared to be the narrowest, I retreated a few steps, gathered myself together, and, after a short run, attempted to take the bog by surprise and get across before it was quite ready to receive me.

Wallowing towards the other side, I felt my feet sinking deeply into the decayed peaty moss, which gurgled expectantly. I was almost over when suddenly, in a second, I sank almost to my waist. Immediately throwing myself on my face, I scrambled forward, and digging my stick into the firm ground in front, pulled for all I was worth. I was almost free when my poor stick broke off with a resounding crack, leaving the top half in my hands. This I again drove into the firm ground, and with a final effort, drew myself out. After a short rest, during which I mourned the loss of my beloved stick, I went on my way determined not to risk a passage over any deceitful bogs in the future unless it was absolutely unavoidable. Very soon the heather became scarcer, and once again I was among dykes and flat, misty, green fields.

For the next two or three hours I ploughed along towards the west, climbing over barbed-wire fences and wading through dykes, unless I was lucky enough to find a plank or small bridge spanning the latter. Scarcely perceptibly the darkness of the eastern sky changed to a dull cold grey and the landscape became clearer, revealing the bare motionless arms of several windmills stretching out into the clearer air, some distance away, in different directions. I roughly judged that I could not be far from the frontier. I might even have crossed it! Though I did my best to suppress undue optimism, this last rather improbable idea persisted in occupying my thoughts.

It is true I had seen nothing recently on the way to arouse suspicion, but, owing to the marshy nature of the country, the guards might well be few and far between. The spirit of approaching dawn lent a faint tinge of colour to the lonely sweeps of white mist drifting slowly above the flat dark fields, and, settling down over the dykes, it commenced to unravel and piece together the ghostly confusion of dim blurred shadows and grossly exaggerated reflections crowding on the smooth, oily surface of the water, until they began to assume a definite shape. I could almost imagine that I was gazing at one of Tingue's early-morning landscapes, so unmistakably Dutch was the scene. Having got thus far no speculations of any sort could be indulged in, the price of uncertainty being too great. A distant village clock chimed four, each beat vibrating clearly in the still air.

The crisis was at hand. Having successfully evaded capture during the eight preceding nights and days, the very thought of failure was unbearable, and compelled me to face the eternal problem of seeking adequate cover for the day at an earlier hour than usual. I therefore commenced a search without delay, experiencing the while, I am convinced, most of the alarming sensations felt by many fat, juicy worms who, having lost their burrows, are endeavouring to avoid contact with all marauding "early birds." The first glance revealed not so much as a bush or hollow willow tree in the immediate vicinity, but in a few minutes I made out a number of heaps of some sort away to the right, through the semi-darkness, so went to make a closer inspection, only to find that two rather broader dykes than usual sought to bar the way.

When on the march a prolonged wetting is naturally most unpleasant, though the continued motion tends to dry one's clothes somewhat by shaking out much of the water. However, there being no alternative, I plunged into the first dyke, which proved to be quite deep, making it again necessary to swim a few strokes. I discovered a plank across the second one, and, passing over, found myself in a stubble field among a number of corn stooks. There being no better cover, I realised that I must hide in one of these little stacks, and chance my luck. The problem was to ascertain which part of the field was least likely to be overrun by people and dogs.

A short inspection showed it to be very long and narrow, while several indications went to prove that the last of the crop had been cut near my original point of entry into the field; this was, therefore, the most desirable part to stay in, as it would naturally be the last to be carried. When people walk through a field they are most liable to wander along near the edges, or go through near the middle; consequently I chose a stook situated between the two, and about thirty yards distant from the end of the field. These heaps were rather too small to form a safe hiding-place, while an unusually large one would, in all probability, attract attention. It is reasonable to suppose that, should a general enlargement be effected embracing a number of stooks in one area, the result would be hardly noticeable. Removing my pack and coat, I set to work transporting two oat sheaves from each of the stooks in the next row for a length of about fifty yards, and adding them to the row in which my nest was planned to be.

To avoid suspicion, I made the now depleted stooks up to their usual strength by again borrowing the same number of sheaves from each of the heaps in the row still further beyond. After repeating this strenuous operation a number of times the desired effect was produced, most of the heaps in my corner of the field now being considerably larger than the rest. Surely it was a good omen that my fat sheaves had devoured many of their leaner brethren, even though the number was not restricted to seven, as in Pharaoh's dream. The value of making oneself as comfortable as possible under adverse conditions cannot be overestimated, for it not only stimulates the instinct of self-preservation, but renders one in the best condition to face the task ahead.

Exposure and fatigue gradually wear down one's powers of resistance and bring with them the feeling that nothing matters. This is to be avoided more than anything, for it introduces the personal element into all reasonings, often forcing a decision against one's better judgment. Having chosen my special heap, I arranged it in such a way as to leave me as much room for movement as possible in the centre. As I exchanged the wetter sheaves for comparatively dry ones, the prospect of once again being warm was delightful and caused me to work with a will. Everything was almost completed, and I was just strewing a little dry straw on the ground between the sheaves, to serve as a mattress, when suddenly a man's voice hailed me, in unmistakable German, from a distance of about fifty yards: "*Was machen sie da?*" ("What are you doing there?"). Any doubts as to which country I was in were rudely dispelled. For a moment I was completely at a loss for an answer, then, bending down, I seized the loose sheaf (which was to have acted as a door to my palace) and placed it against the others, and, turning round, replied in low German, "I am only replacing these, which have fallen down."

Two workmen were standing just beyond the dyke, having evidently approached by an unobserved track, and were now gazing suspiciously at me. There being no more prostrate sheaves, I could not very well throw some down and then pick them up again, for the action would not have been at all convincing. I therefore had to content myself with smoothing the side of the stook in a business-like way, trusting that the uncertain light would not disclose the insanity of my actions. In a few seconds I moved to another stook, and was commencing to stroke the sheaves, when the same voices demanded, in a peremptory manner, to know what I was really doing. It was a case of bluff, so, busying myself with the heap, I snapped out, "*Ach!* go away, I have a lot to do."

From the murmur that reached me it was obvious that this abrupt answer was puzzling them considerably. My position was still extremely unsafe, for border folk are usually of a very suspicious nature, which is intensified by the activities of war. At the best of times my excuse would have been feeble enough. Ordinary people don't usually rise at four a.m. for the purpose of walking round a soaking field stroking sheaves of corn. Besides, it was not unlikely that I was talking to the owner of the field.

Whether they saw the brass buttons on my service jacket, or merely felt that I was wanted, I do not know, but they walked quickly towards the plank spanning the dyke which divided their field from mine. Directly they reached it one of them shouted something that I could not understand and was immediately answered by a third person, away in the mist. Once across the plank the men, after jabbering excitedly, came towards me at a quick run. Needless to say, it is extremely dangerous to be chased in bare country of this sort just when the day is breaking and the fields rapidly filling with workers, for once the alarm is raised the result is almost certain to mean capture. This time, however, it was not a matter of choice; my hand had been forced, compelling me reluctantly to play my last card.

Picking up my pack and coat, I ran as only once before in my varied career—the night when I almost felt the pitchforks belonging to the little devils which chased me away from Ströhen camp. After running about a hundred yards, trusting to the mist and uncertain light to partially screen my movements, I turned aside and dived headlong into a stook, pulling the straw after me. In a few seconds my pursuers drew level and, to my intense satisfaction, passed on, breathing heavily. This is the last I saw of these two eager sons of the Fatherland. For all I know, they may be still following the excellent example afforded by *Charlie's Aunt*.

CHAPTER 11

Holland

I was now in a small wet stook, very cold and hungry. It being too light to risk a return journey to my carefully prepared nest, I had to take things as they were, and fell to wondering what it must feel like to be in a nice warm bed. The day proved to be one long nightmare. By careful observation I saw that a number of girls were working on the same crop, luckily at the other end of the field. They appeared only to be gleaning, but as it was quite likely this was preparatory to the carting, I resolved to keep a very sharp look-out to avoid being transfixed by a pitchfork and hoisted on to a cart. About breakfast-time a peculiar noise came from somewhere quite close, so, parting the corn carefully, I peered out in that direction. There, to my horror, were three men scything the rushes along a ditch which passed a few feet from me. The heap was a small one, and, therefore, to avoid detection, I endeavoured to put the best part of it between myself and them when they were working the closest to me.

The completion of this operation naturally left me a little exposed on what I supposed to be my safe side. The men had almost passed, when I happened to look away from the ditch and saw a farmer standing beside the very next heap to mine, surveying the crop, his hands in his pockets. Somehow or other I wriggled back unobserved, and lay shivering with a combination of cold and fear. After half-an-hour's wait, I again looked out cautiously, and was relieved to find the man gone, though there seemed to be even more people in the neighbourhood than before. To add to my discomfort the breeze increased to quite a strong, piercing wind, which whistled in and out among the corn-sheaves until I felt very like an ice-cream in a refrigerator.

Even then there were more trials to come, for, not only did the grain pour itself into my clothes, eyes and ears, but also mixed with the crop was a large proportion of barley or bearded wheat, which took a truly fiendish delight in slowly but relentlessly making its way up my sleeves or down my back. In this predicament it seemed almost unthinkable that I should ever have been so foolish in my schooldays as to pick barley heads and deliberately put them a little way up my coat-sleeves, the barbs downwards, expressly for the pleasure of feeling them crawling up my arms. Most of us do curious things in our youth!

Suffice it to say that, in spite of all convictions to the contrary, I was still in the heap, unmolested, when the afternoon resolved itself into evening and the labourers left for their homes. A little before nine o'clock, after a short but drenching shower, I could stand it no longer, so crawled out, damp and cold, but still almost glad to be alive. Looking towards the west in the fading light, I saw a large shape moving slowly from left to right through the country, roughly a couple of miles away. It could only be a sail. With a sinking feeling I realised that in front lay at least one more canal which must be crossed. (This canal, I afterwards discovered, was actually in Holland.) Although I did not feel desperately hungry, I somehow felt that I was getting near the end of my tether; my food, also, was dwindling and could not last more than two days at the outside, for I was already half-way through my emergency ration, a tin of Quaker oats. Strange to say, porridge is nothing like as nice eaten raw.

As soon as it was dark I started out, resolved not only to be extremely cautious, but, at the same time, to get as far as possible before the next day overtook me, time now threatening to form one of my most formidable adversaries. Travelling across country, I soon came upon a long road bordered by trees, so hid in the edge of some beans to make sure that all was clear before venturing across it. Almost immediately I heard voices not far distant, and presently a man on a bicycle rode past. When everything was quiet again I managed to step across the road unobserved, feeling sure that another danger point was past. The night being cold it may be imagined that I was scarcely overjoyed at finding it necessary to wade or swim through another short series of dykes; this was, however, the case.

Drawing near to the dreaded canal, I noticed that on either flank, some distance away, were clusters of rather brilliant lights. Presumably this pointed to the fact that these lights were placed at points of special importance, such as strongly guarded bridges, in which case it seemed probable that the canal might form part of the boundary line. In order to avoid the slightest rustle which might attract attention, I rolled my raincoat and secured it over one shoulder, "*bandolier* fashion." I next covered the brass buttons of my tunic with mud, to prevent their reflecting the rays of a possible flashlight, and, after smearing some dirt on my face and hands, moved forward once more, prepared, in case of discovery, to make a dash towards the west regardless of the consequences.

In a few minutes I saw, by the even line of the higher ground in front, that I had almost reached the raised canal, and was just preparing to mount the short, grassy slope when I came upon a hard-worn narrow track running along near the edge of a rather wide dyke, which separated me from the embankment. The dyke being in the lee of the wind it seemed advisable to ascertain whether it was possible to cross by any plank or bridge which might be in the vicinity in preference to going through it, for, though one may be able to get into a dyke quietly enough, the getting out is a very different matter when the sides are steep and one's clothes full of water. Walking along this path very warily for about twenty yards, I was lucky enough to discover a plank leading across (for except for the faint silhouette of the top of the embankment against the sky, practically everything was hidden by the darkness). Though the plank bent threateningly I succeeded in crossing it, and crawled to the top of the rise.

A glance revealed a broad, reed-fringed canal, reflecting little dancing lights on its wind-swept surface—the stars which had the audacity to peep out from between the clouds. I could hear the splashings of a water-rat actually swimming at that time of night for the fun of it! Quickly crossing the tow-path and parting the reeds, I followed its example, and, not waiting to remove pack, clothing or shoes, swam towards the opposite bank as silently as possible. It can only have been a few yards across, but I remember feeling almost as tired as if I had swum the Channel. This was the tenth night of my escapade, and the strain was certainly beginning to tell. As I was leaving the canal behind some wild duck rose from a dyke close by me, with much flapping of wings. If their desire was to frighten me they certainly achieved their object.

When, after an hour or more, I continued plodding along without seeing anything unusual, I could not help again wondering if I was still in German territory. My curiosity increased when two motor cycles with powerful headlights went by on what appeared to be a main road. I had not seen anything like that for weeks, so resolved to go along the road myself in the hope of seeing some other strange sights. Immediately on arriving there I had to take cover in a corner of an orchard to avoid another light, which was rapidly overtaking me. From this point of vantage I was soon able to see that the light was on a bicycle, and the rider not a tin soldier, complete with helmet and curling moustache, but a peaceably dressed young woman. Encouraged by the promising trend of events, I stole some apples and made my way, munching and shivering, towards a little group of houses, hoping to discover some writing which might prove which country I was in.

Eventually I found a letter-box and feverishly endeavoured to decipher, in the semi-darkness, a long word printed in black letters on a white background. With a sinking heart I slowly made out the letters B—R—I—E. Was it necessary to read any further? Surely this was proof positive that I was still under the gentle sway of the *Kaiser!* What else could the remainder be but "*feasten*," completing the German word for letter-box. With almost a feeling of resignation, I continued to wrest the remaining letters from the darkness. The expected F was a very peculiar shape. No, it was a V, after all! With every letter my hopes rose as I spelt out the remaining E N B U S. I do not profess to be a German scholar, but I do know that the word "*Brievenbus*" does not adorn their letter-boxes in the ordinary course of events. Feeling vaguely happy, but still haunted by the first syllable of the word, I made my way further into the village.

At first all seemed quiet, but presently I heard a couple talking near the entrance of a house. Creeping up as close as I dared in the deep shadow of the building, I strained my ears almost to dislocation to catch a few words of the conversation. The language they were speaking struck me as peculiarly ugly, and did not seem to lend itself readily to the uses to which they were undoubtedly putting it. The fact that they were not speaking ordinary German did not necessarily mean that the language was Dutch, for it might have been some border dialect. However, I could restrain myself no longer, so, walking up to the man, I addressed him thus in German, with as much nonchalance as I could command: "Can you tell me if I am in Germany or Holland?"

He did not seem to grasp the question at once, which in itself was a good sign, though it lengthened my breathless suspense. I believe I would willingly have murdered him if, by doing so, I could have had the answer an instant sooner, for so much depended on it. All at once he straightened himself up and, in a surprised voice, replied, "Holland!"

I should never have believed that one simple word could have meant so much. The news so completely overwhelmed me that, for a few seconds, I failed to grasp its import. Then, springing forward, I seized and shook his hand so violently that it almost threatened to fall off, at the same time showering explanations at him in a hundred and one different languages, in the hope that he would understand one of them. Needless to say, at first the unfortunate Dutchman was rather perturbed at being so cordially greeted by someone he must have thought to be a dangerous lunatic at large, though I consider that he stood the ordeal very well. I think the girl was the first to really grasp the situation, for, to my surprise, she congratulated me in broken German, and insisted on shaking hands, too.

In spite of the good news I was still wet, cold and hungry, and the prospect of again sleeping in a warm bed was very alluring. I therefore inquired the way to the nearest hotel, and was told to make for a larger village, some three kilometres distant. I asked if there was any possibility of my taking a wrong turn leading back into Hunland, and being assured there was none if I followed the main road, started off in the best of spirits. It was just like walking on air. My dreams of freedom had at last come true. Though it was after one o'clock, I encountered several people and each time inquired the way, thus making assurance doubly sure. I can hardly attempt to describe the strange exultant feelings which surged through me as I marched along, conscious of having left "Brother Bosch" behind.

Eventually, singing a marching song, I rounded a corner and found myself in a village street, almost opposite a house in front of which hung a sign, just distinguishable in the darkness: "*Hotel Van Dijk.*" Regardless of the fact that I did not possess a cent, I proceeded to knock loudly on the front door. After a few minutes my efforts were rewarded by hearing an upstairs window open, and being told in Dutch to go away. However, my mind being made up, I persisted in making more noise than ever. Seeing his protestations were in vain, and evidently scenting something unusual, I understood "*mein Host*" to say that he would come down. My knowledge of the laws of internment of a neutral country being very limited, it behoved me to act with extreme caution if I wished to follow in the footsteps of brother escapers, whom I knew had preceded me to England.

Though I had committed no act of war, such as crossing the frontier carrying arms, I did not feel very sure of my ground. Therefore when the elderly innkeeper, holding a flickering candle, shot back the bolts, he found me wearing only a khaki shirt and grey flannel trousers, the soaking raincoat and tunic having been hurriedly secreted in my pack, so that he could not assert that I was in uniform when he first saw me, in case the subject should be raised later. As soon as he heard the facts of the case, the Dutchman motioned me to accompany him along the street, which I did wonderingly. I imagined myself shortly being interviewed by a fat, sleepy-eyed and pompous *burgomaster*, who would either fall upon my neck, or order me straight back to Germany.

After half-an-hour's walk, when my guide halted beside a long wooden hut and knocked vigorously, I decided that there was nothing to fear in that direction, for no such distinguished person would deign to live in so humble a residence. Presently, in answer to our repeated efforts, we heard several grumbling voices, a door was opened, and I was bidden to enter. As soon as I was accustomed to the glaring gas-light, I experienced a considerable shock. Occupying the whole length of the room in which I stood was a double line of beds, mostly containing sleeping men, and from the walls hung many greenish uniforms, rifles and bayonets! On recovering from my first surprise, I turned to a fully dressed soldier I took to be a sergeant, who by this time, presumably, understood that I was an escaped "*Inglesman*," and asked him, in German, for an explanation.

In the midst of his almost unintelligible reply I caught the word "*Grenswacht*" (frontier guard). Seeing that we were at cross purposes, the sergeant roused a man who spoke very fair English and acted as interpreter. I soon learnt that I was in the local headquarters of the Dutch Frontier Guard, and would have to remain there until seen by an officer the next day. This suited me only too well, so having duly impressed the fact that I was not in uniform, I retired to a bed arranged for me in the N.C.O.'s room, and commenced to pull off my wet clothes.

Meanwhile tongues had not been idle, and eager, curious faces began to peep at the "stray dog" through the half-open door. Just as I was about to turn in, curiosity could be restrained no longer; the room filled with noisy young fellows, who took up a position round my bed and proceeded to bombard me with questions. It was all so well meant that I endeavoured to give them a brief outline of my doings, in German. The idea of an Englishman speaking German was evidently quite beyond their comprehension, for, judging by many doubtful looks of astonishment, it seemed that the general impression was that

I was a camouflaged Hun. As they all persisted in talking at once, I put an end to the argument by disappearing under the bedclothes. About ten o'clock the next morning I awoke, feeling stiffer than ever before, the slightest contraction of a muscle resembling the jerking of a rusty wire. However, when a soldier, seeing that I was awake, brought my breakfast, I sat up with remarkable agility and devoured every crumb.

Never have I enjoyed a meal more. Every additional mouthful of the deliciously fresh Dutch cheese and new bread seemed to receive a still more exquisite taste when I thought of the Irish stew I had missed when standing behind my imitation wall at Ströhen. It was not until after a thoroughly good scrub and a cold bath that I could screw up enough courage to look at myself in a mirror, and, prepared as I was, the sudden reflection of the wild-eyed, bearded tramp considerably surprised me. A little before lunch, having obtained some dry under-clothing, I was sitting on my bed, extracting a selection of barbed wire and splinters from my hands with a large needle, when a Dutch officer walked in to see the curiosity. He greeted me cordially in very good English, introducing himself as Lieutenant Hoffman, in charge of the local detachment of the Frontier Guard, and asked me to lunch with him at his hotel.

On the way thither I could not help being very impressed by the design and beauty of the village. The houses were mostly large, with spacious, well-kept gardens, the streets clean and the general atmo-sphere of the place spoke of great prosperity. Hoffman took me to a barber, who performed for a long time, but in the end turned out a comparatively respectable human being. At lunch I met another Dutch officer, also an English scholar, who, after hearing the latter part of my experience, told me that I must have actually walked along the Ger-man sentry's path, just beyond the canal, the night before. Having had no escaped prisoners in that district before, they had a disquieting idea that I should very likely be interned. I learnt that, in all probability, I should proceed to a larger town for further examination the following day, and gathered that, in the meantime, it would be advisable for me to remain close to my headquarters and refrain from wandering about by myself, the frontier being too close for safety.

Shortly after lunch the two officers entered the room, carrying a couple of sporting guns, and announced their intention of spending the afternoon at a canal on the frontier duck shooting, and said that I might expect them back about teatime. Being a prisoner no longer the very thought of seeing grey-clad sentries standing at their posts appealed to me so much that I begged to be allowed to accompany them, deciding to run the small risk such a visit might entail. Hoffman was considerably surprised at my proposal, but said I could come at my own risk if I thought I had known him long enough to be able to take his word. He reminded me, at the same time, that one can easily step over a frontier line, intentionally or otherwise, and produced a loaded automatic pistol from his coat pocket as if to back up his argument, asking me to choose my course of action. For a few seconds I reasoned with myself and then accepted, it seeming perfectly obvious that Hoffman would never have shown his hand had he intended playing a crooked game. Just before starting the innkeeper lent me a civilian cap and overcoat, which gave me a sense of security and enabled me to set out with the others if not a perfect, at any rate a passable Dutchman.

Presently we arrived at a bridge-head, where the Dutch guard turned out and saluted, when, it must be confessed, I felt a trifle nervous, being then almost on the frontier. The formalities over, we left our bicycles in the guardroom and, crossing the bridge, proceeded along the tow-path at the side of the canal. There, sure enough, were the grey-clad sentries, standing near their boxes along a little raised path, at intervals varying from one to two hundred yards. Seeing that our presence seemed to occasion considerable interest on the part of the sentries, I inquired the reason from one of my companions, and was informed that only persons in the company of Dutch officers were allowed where we were walking, in the neutral zone dividing the two countries.

Curiously enough the water dog, whose duty it was to start the birds from among the reeds, was English and went by the name of "Tom." Fortunately he was very obedient, for had he once crossed between the extenuated lines of grey men Tom would have afforded the Huns some moving target practice, which in all probability would have resulted in his contributing to a sausage machine. I am sure I do not know what I should have done if this had happened while I was with the party, for Tom, when feeling lonely, used to run straight up to me, wagging his stumpy tail and looking up with eyes which so plainly said that he was indeed glad to meet a fellow-countryman, for, though Dutchmen were kind enough to him, the scent was somewhat different.

Towards the end of the afternoon we came to a place where the frontier line gradually converged, running parallel to, and about twenty-five yards away from, the canal, just the other side of a dyke at the bottom of the embankment. It must have been somewhere here that an unseen hand had unconsciously guided me to safety through the darkness of the night before. I selected a particularly Hunnish-looking sentry, who was standing beside a painted black and white box, with a long, wicked-looking and old-patterned bayonet gleaming above his slung rifle, and, hailing him casually, remarked that it must be weary work doing nothing, and inquired if he was tired of the war, to which he replied with a sullen "*Ja.*" Undismayed by his dismal expression, I inquired if they ever had any escaped prisoners in those parts. This time he did not deign to answer, but merely shook his head solemnly. By removing my coat I could have easily disillusioned him, but, re-membering that a rifle bullet is not a thing to be trifled with, I re-frained.

Feeling my triumph complete, I turned and limped away, still hardly able to realise that only a few hours before I had unknowingly paraded along the same little raised path which the Germans were so jealously guarding. Of all my escapes this was the most inexplicable. To what was it due? Certainly not to my own initiative alone. Man's extremity is indeed God's opportunity.

★★★★★★

Supreme in the world of red tape, far above the ken of misguided mortals, lives an omnipotent being—the Censor. In imagination, he sits in a huge armchair, wreathed in tobacco smoke, casually sorting, from piles of manuscript, the sheep from the goats. The former are destined to be smothered in official stamps and coloured inks, while the latter are cast ignominiously into the gigantic waste-paper basket. Though this little sheep, in particular, may have a little of its wool shorn off, I trust that it may eventually avoid the rubbish heap. For this reason I must ask the reader to be contented with a very curtailed and disjointed account of the remainder of my wanderings.

★★★★★★

In due course I was placed in a quarantine camp, to remain there until a given number of days should elapse, when, on being pro-nounced free from infection, I should be allowed to continue my journey through Holland. The camp contained a number of German deserters who, it appeared, crossed the frontier in this district at the average rate of one *per diem*, having for the most part arrived direct from the front, with every intention of leaving their beloved "*Vater-land*" behind forever. They made no secret of the fact that they hoped to be able to emigrate to England or America as soon as it was all over. Several of them were N.C.O.'s, wearing the black and white ribbon of the Iron Cross, to all appearances good soldiers whom their relentless system had forced to desertion rather than the terror of the British guns. The Germans occupied a separate hut, and were kept strictly to themselves. This probably saved a lot of trouble, for, judging by the spirited way they occasionally sang "*Deutschland, Deutschland über alles,*" accompanied by an accordion, the spirit of patriotism and savage "*kultur*" still flowed in their veins.

Doubtless the first German band to return to England will be composed of the most gentle peace and beer-loving Huns that ever visited our favoured shores. Whatever the nature of the welcome and guarantees extended to them by our English "Bolsheviks" (who even now have the audacity to advocate a policy of "shake and be friends"),their lives will not be at all secure when they come in contact, as they ultimately must, with Britishers who have been most brutally treated and forced to work as prisoners in the German salt mines, men who have come to know the truth of the saying, "*Once a Bosch, always a Bosch,*" during their stay of several years in Hunland. I feel genuinely sorry for the very few really nice Germans who certainly do exist (several of whom I met during my captivity). However, considering that their influence has been practically *nil* in the war, on account of their being in such a minority, I suppose they will be bound to suffer with the rest.

The number of escaped French and Russian soldiers was surprising. However they must have had many excellent opportunities, while working in the fields near the frontier, to cross the dividing line. It did not take me long to discover three British privates, who were distinctly bored and very pleased to see me. The eldest was a South African, escaped from a reprisal camp, while the other two belonged to the Warwicks. Though little more than boys they had in all probability seen more of the hardships of life than many men of treble their age. Great excitement prevailed when, by dint of much cajoling, I managed to procure a *mandoline* from the town, for, though the meals were very much looked forward to and enjoyed, the rest of the time passed very slowly. It is not easy to play tunes to satisfy the cravings of different nationalities at a moment's notice.

A few Russians flung themselves about to the lilt of some of their rowdiest cake-walks, while the "*Marseillaise*," seeming a universal favourite, was repeatedly called for. On the morning of the fourth day three weird-looking figures, wearing a queer mixture of ready-made Dutch garments, entered the camp with a guard. I could scarcely believe my eyes when I recognised some of my former companions at Ströhen. Two of them, Captain Harrison, of the Royal Irish, and Lieutenant C. F. Templar, 1st Gloucesters (since then, I regret to say, killed in action), were "old Contemptibles," having been captured about the beginning of the war, while the third, Lieutenant J. Insall, V.C., R.F.C., had been in captivity two years. They had all made many previous attempts to escape, and consequently had sampled many German prisons, and now at last succeeded.

Captain Harrison, I have since heard, was again captured, during the German advance in the spring of '18, but was fortunately able to regain our lines the same night. Our delight at meeting again outside Germany was mutual, and, having so many notes to exchange, the time then passed much more rapidly. After various communications with the British authorities, we were successful at last in getting in touch with the British Minister at the Hague, who almost immediately obtained our release from the quarantine camp, to the unbounded astonishment of the local Dutch magnates.

★★★★★★

Receiving an invitation to visit Sir Walter Townley (British Minister), I proceeded to the Hague, freed at last from the annoying formality of being continually escorted by an officer or guard. Imagine my pleasure at once more sitting down to afternoon tea in an English drawing-room. I shall never forget the kind thought and solicitude of my hostess, Lady Susan. I almost seemed to be in England.

Before catching my train back, I engaged a taxi and tried to see as much of the town as possible in the time. The driver understood but little of my directions; the sight, however, of a few *guldens* caused him to drive so recklessly that I thought my last hour had come. It seemed that we must be leaving the path strewn with luckless victims. Arriving at the Palace of Peace, where the nations had so unsuccessfully beguiled each other with "smooth words, softer than honey," I succeeded in inducing my charioteer to come to a standstill. Alighting, a policeman informed me that the building had just been closed, but pointed out the highly ornamental metal gates, which, at the cost of 40,000 *marks*, had been presented by the Kaiser Wilhelm a few years before the war.

Espying on them angels of peace carrying palm branches, I could contain myself no longer, so delivered an impassioned harangue to the astonished Dutchman on the subject of hypocrisy, in a mixture of German, French and Dutch. Presently, seeing a large crowd gathering around us, I concluded my remarks with a substantial tip, and signalling to *Mynheer Mercury*, was once more whirled into space.

★★★★★★

The convoy, in formation, steamed through the neutral waters towards the open sea. On board were a party of women and children, proceeding from Germany to England for repatriation. Several of them must have been in Germany an exceedingly long time, for they could only speak broken English, while some of the children, having evidently been born there, could speak no English at all. Soon the ship began to roll gently in response to the ever-increasing swell. As the White Ensign fluttered happily from the stern, most of us took advantage of the still comparatively calm sea by parading along the deck in company with a British commodore, confidently straining our eyes to catch a first glimpse of the approaching escort; and it was, unfortunately, obvious that everyone on board did not share our good spirits.

As the disconcerting movements of the ship increased, the Anglo-German element, pale-faced and dejected, assembled amidships, and forming a small, huddled group, hastily commenced to put on their cork jackets and life-belts, evidently preparing for the expected impact of the dreaded torpedo. Just then, as the look-out, attracted by some specks of foam emerging from the grey, misty horizon, signalled that a number of ships were fast approaching, they could stand the strain no longer, so, breaking into a weird German chant, they wailed disconsolately. Could it be that the victorious German fleet, of which they had so often heard, was at this very moment bearing down upon us? Perish the thought! The specks of white grew larger with alarming rapidity.

It was not until the British destroyer flotilla was almost on us that we could discern, behind each dividing mass of curving foam, the sinister and capable grey shapes of Britannia's watch-dogs moving swiftly, in perfect harmony with sea and sky. As if inspired by one mind, our guardians turned about, and silently taking up their respective positions at a reduced speed, they passed with us safely along the King's Highway!